The Women's Health BIG BOOK *of* YOGA

RODALE.

© 2012 by Kathryn Budig

First published as a trade paperback by Rodale Inc. in September 2012.

This 2014 edition printed for Barnes & Noble, Inc.

All rights reserved. No part of this publication may be reproduced or transmitted in any form or by any means, electronic or mechanical,
including photocopying, recording, or any other information storage and retrieval system,
without the written permission of the publisher.

Rodale books may be purchased for business or promotional use or for special sales.
For information, please write to: Special Markets Department, Rodale Inc., 733 3rd Ave, New York, NY 10017

Women's Health is a registered trademark of Rodale Inc.

Printed in China
Rodale Inc. makes every effort to use acid-free ♾, recycled paper ♻.

Book design by Laura White
With George Karabotsos, design director of *Men's Health* and *Women's Health* Books

Photo editor: Mark Haddad

All photography by Beth Bischoff

Cover stylist: Anna Su
Cover hairstylist and makeup: Robert Huitron

Library of Congress Cataloging-in-Publication Data is on file with the publisher.

ISBN-13: 978–1–4351–5849–8 paperback

2 4 6 8 10 9 7 5 3 1   trade paperback

We inspire and enable people to improve their lives and the world around them.
rodalebooks.com

Contents

For my father, who taught me that anything is possible.

Acknowledgments

I wouldn't be writing this book without the love and support of Michele Promaulayko. You are an inspiration, a role model, and an amazing friend. Your support means the world to me. Also thanks to Dave Zinczenko and Steve Perrine.

A huge thanks to photographer Beth Bischoff for making my book a visual feast and for keeping things real. Anna Su, you are a stylish inspiration; Robert Huitron, you make magic happen with hair and makeup. Thank you to George Karabostsos and Laura White for making my book come alive and keeping us laughing on set.

This certainly wouldn't be *The Big Book of Yoga* without my amazing models (and dear friends) who blew me away with their beauty and talent. Mary Clare Aeillo, Faith Hunter, Giselle Mari, Leo Marrs, and MacKenzie Miller—you honor me by being in my book.

To my fantastic editor, Ursula Cary. You're a true yogi. Thanks also to the rest of the Rodale team, especially Erin Williams, Nancy Elgin, and Erana Bumbardatore.

Big love to my team that keeps me alive and well: Danielle Lindberg, Amy Stanton, and Eric Greenspan. I'd be lost without you.

For your faith in me: Melinda Fishman and Eileen Opatut.

My amazing contributors for their expertise and time: Kia Miller, Gary Goldman, Rod Stryker, Debbie Kim, Gina Caputo, Jill Miller, Heather Seineger, Annie Carpenter, and Jason Wachob. Much love to triple threat Tiffany Cruikshank—book model, contributor, and friend.

Thanks to Elisabeth Rogani, Lululemon, Beyond Yoga, Champion, KiraGrace, Adidas, Alex and Ani, Maria Melinda, and Brandy Melville for the amazing outfits and jewelry! Deep gratitude for my teachers and guides along the way: Maty Ezraty, Chuck Miller, Heath House, Seane Corn, Noah Maze, my Yogaglo family, and all of my students around the world.

To my dog, Ashi. For spending hours patiently staring at me as I type away, knowing snuggles, snacks, and walks are around the corner. You remind me that everything is made out of love and that there is always something to be joyful for.

To my phenomenal family and friends—you are the core of everything I do. Thank you to my beautiful mother and father for supporting every dream I've ever had. Love to my brother and sister and their families.

For my friends—Ashley Swider-Cebulka, Elli Boland, Casey Van Zandt, Karly Wade, Keith Levin, and Caroline Shea—your laughter and hours spent discussing life keeps me whole, inspired, and ready to take on the world.

And lastly, thank you to my partner and love of my life, Bob. For your dedication, advice, belief, love, and always reminding me to reach for the sky.

Introduction

I lived in Los Angeles for 8 years—the mecca for slender, beautiful, "perfect" people. But take a closer look behind all the glitz, glamour, and designer sunglasses and you'll find a lot of very beautiful, unhappy people. The cutthroat world of Hollywood is especially tough on women, which I experienced firsthand. I arrived in Los Angeles at the ripe age of 21, hoping to pursue my dreams of acting while teaching yoga on the side to keep me going from gig to gig. I remember my first meeting with a manager like it was yesterday. She took one look at my frame—all 5'2" and 108 pounds—and told me that I could be the funny best friend. If I ever wanted to play the ingenue I'd have to drop at least 10 pounds.

I went home feeling confused and hurt.

Was I fat? I'm not attractive or slim enough to play a lead? I always thought I was in such good shape. Do I need to diet? Start drinking coffee and smoke cigarettes? Everything made me cringe. The uncomfortable questions went on and on, but my yoga practice answered all of my questions. My teachers kept reminding me that I was perfect exactly as I was—and I was fit and slim thanks to my daily practice. More importantly, yoga reminded me that life is about balance and not extremes. Life is meant to be enjoyed and embraced along with all of the discipline and challenges that it presents. Yoga showed me that self-acceptance and belief in myself was the key to strength and beauty.

In retrospect, that audition was a

complete blessing because it guided me into an "accidental career" of teaching yoga full-time. I learned at a young age that the only way to experience happiness is by taking chances and following what makes my heart beat. Every minute I spend training and teaching is me at my best. It puts a smile on my face every single day. I hope to empower you through yoga to find what makes your heart beat. Practicing yoga allows you to connect to your untapped potential. Whether it's mastering a handstand or allowing a simple savasana to chill you out at the end of the day, yoga offers unlimited potential to be your best self.

I teach yoga because it works. I practice yoga because it completes me. I've written this book with the hope that you'll be tempted to do the same—live the life you've always wanted. Reclaim that strong, calm, powerful spirit within. Heal old injuries, whether physical or mental— and have an insanely fun time!

Enjoy your journey. Remember that it takes valleys to create peaks! These poses and sequences are here to make you feel fantastic, to challenge you to be the best version of yourself, and to keep you healthy, fit, and beautiful. Rock your practice, and make it yours. Often all it takes is a good group of Sun Salutations or a fabulous inversion to remind you how unique and strong you are. As one of my favorite men of all time put so well, "Be yourself; everyone else is already taken." —Oscar Wilde

Namaste, y'all.

xo Kathryn

CHAPTER 1

Ready, Set, Om
Your transformation starts here

I

f you picked up this
book, you're probably one of three types of people:
either you're curious about yoga, you want to
deepen your practice, or you're just a sucker for
pretty pictures. No matter which type you are, you'll
find what you're looking for here. And even if you're
a beginner, the truth is that you've already begun
your yoga practice, simply by intending to make
yoga a part of your life. I promise, it will be worth it.

Ready, Set, Om

"Yoga," which in Sanskrit translates to "yoke," "union," or "discipline," has persevered for thousands of years. It's had enough face lifts and transformations to make even Madonna look like a slacker. While the main focus of this book is on how we interpret yoga in the West today—as a challenging workout that tones your muscles, calms your mind, and strengthens your spirit—it's important to understand its roots, too.

One of my teachers once said of yoga, "The more you learn, you realize the less you know." Yoga will teach you how to unify your mind, body, and soul, leaving you refreshed, calm, and ready to take on the world (or, rather, one awesome moment of life at a time). It does this by strengthening and lengthening your body, slowing down your mind, and opening up your perspective. Welcome to the journey of a lifetime! Let's start with a little background.

A Land before Sports Clubs

The original hard-core yogis weren't kidding around when it came to practicing yoga. Their goal was to discover their true natures and embrace the process of transformation without expectation or attachment to the results. Essentially, they were trying to be at one in their minds, bodies, and souls. The best way for them to cultivate this lifestyle 3,500 years ago was to completely detach themselves from civilization and spend every moment dedicated to this process. While living in a remote cave with no cell phone reception is a one-way ticket to a meltdown in the modern world, these yogis found solitude crucial to calming their minds and steadying their focus.

I don't expect you to completely change your daily routine, but it's a good idea to make time to take care of yourself—whether you do that by taking a lunchtime yoga class or just by taking 15 minutes to quietly relax and close your eyes. Even the smallest bit of relaxation makes a big difference! According to a 2011 study in the *Scandinavian Journal of Work, Environment, and Health,* participation in a 6-week yoga intervention program was associated with improvements in well-being and resilience to stress.

In that study, a group of employees at a British university participated in six 1-hour yoga classes over the course of 6 weeks. At the end of the study, they reported higher levels of well-being than did control group members, who did not attend yoga classes. Participants assessed themselves using the Profile of Mood States Bipolar Scale and the Inventory of Positive Psychological Attitudes. Those in the yoga group scored higher on clear-mindedness, composure, elation, energy, and confidence. They also reported increased life purpose and satisfaction, as well as feelings of greater self-confidence during stressful situations. So, taking the time out of your busy day to do yoga is worth it!

Asanas—"comfortable seats," in Sanskrit—are the yoga postures. The original form of yoga consisted of plenty of sitting and meditation—a little different from the sweat-inducing vinyasa classes we see in the movies. Gurus (see page 000) taught that the self (our egos) must be sacrificed in order to attain happiness and liberation from the dregs of life that weigh us down. The intensity of sacrifice espoused evolved into a set of standards, or rules, to live by for those who were willing to dedicate their lives to yoga.

The Eight Limbs of Yoga

Possibly the most famous yoga philosopher went by the name of Patanjali. This guy is celebrated as the father of yoga. His personal history is shrouded in mystery and myth, so I actually like to call him the Godfather. Patanjali penned the famous *Yoga Sutras* in the 2nd century BC. These are 195 statements on how to conduct oneself in life in order to achieve enlightenment. He was the creator of the eight-limbed path of yoga (referred to as "ashtanga yoga"), which frees one from physical, mental, and emotional suffering when followed properly.

Patanjali's sutras formed a yoga to-do list that includes yamas (restraints), niyamas (disciplines), asanas (physical postures), pranayama (breath control), pratyahara (withdrawal of the senses), dharana (concentration), dhyana (meditation), and samadhi (liberation). The words may seem complicated and tricky to pronounce, but don't get too overwhelmed. Think of them as a basic guide to being a good person. They're just suggestions for how to deal with the everyday stresses in life—kind of like a nonreligious Ten Commandments. When you feel good about yourself, that positive energy translates throughout the rest of your life.

The Yamas

The yamas—or restraints—set out to give the yogi a solid ethical foundation. The *Yoga Sutras* identify the five yamas as ahimsa (nonviolence), satya (truthfulness), asetya (nonstealing), brahmacharya (abstinence), and aparigraha (nongreed). The question is, what do they all mean and how do you use them? Let's break them down.

AHIMSA (nonviolence)

This can have a multitude of definitions and echoes the commandment "Thou shalt not kill." While it clearly prescribes practicing self-restraint when you feel like taking out your boss or mother-in-law, it stresses living compassionately in general. Anger is a rash emotion, and violence often follows it. Being in tune with one's thoughts and actions helps the yogi to chill with the anger and harbor no hatred. Ahimsa also means that we can't be violent toward ourselves, including in the way we treat our bodies and how we deal with injury, and that our bodies must be honored as the sacred temples they are.

SATYA (truthfulness)

Literally translated as "don't lie," this yama insists that we speak the truth even when we think it's easier to hide

THE FIRST LADY OF YOGA

In the 1930s, Russian-born Indra Devi caused quite the stir. The Mysore royal family insisted that Krishnamacharya teach her (yes, a woman!), and he grudgingly agreed. After proving herself beyond worthy, they became friends and she went on to introduce yoga in the Soviet Union, Argentina, and China, where she opened a school in Shanghai. Her popularity grew. She opened a studio in Los Angeles and taught leading ladies Marilyn Monroe and Greta Garbo. This powerhouse passed away in April 2002, but she left an inspiring legacy for women everywhere.

Ready, Set, Om

behind falsehoods. It directs us to be thoughtful with our words and to always speak with intention.

ASETYA (nonstealing)

This aligns with the commandments not to steal or covet what others have. We've all been taught from a young age that stealing is wrong, but longing to possess someone else's success or existence is just as bad. As mythologist and scholar Joseph Campbell so eloquently said, "The privilege of a lifetime is being who you are," and I have a feeling Patanjali would back that up. Longing for what we lack causes suffering, but being comfortable with what we have and who we are creates stability and happiness.

BRAHMACHARYA (abstinence)

This one makes the modern-day yogi twitch. Patanjali definitely meant celibacy, which doesn't quite jibe with today's lifestyles—or any episode of *Sex in the City*, for that matter! His thoughts were that sexual energy took away from the focus one could put toward devotion. I prefer to translate it this way: Avoid using your sexuality recklessly. Offer your sexuality to those who deserve it and will respect you, so you can respect yourself, in turn.

WHAT YOU'LL NEED

While yoga is mainly practiced with only a mat, there are additional props you may want to have on hand to experiment with and deepen your practice. These yoga props can be ordered online at sites like Gaiam.com, Manduka.com, and Yogitoes.com; you often can also find good deals at your local T.J.Maxx or Marshalls.

TWO YOGA BLOCKS

These come in foam, cork, or bamboo. They're often used to lie on, so test out the different textures to see what your body responds to. Whatever you buy, make sure they're sturdy so they can hold as much weight as you choose to place on them.

USES
- Supporting the bridge pose
- Supporting a headstand
- Opening the chest
- Aiding flexibility in standing poses

STRETCHY STRAP

A circle strap made out of stretchy, adjustable fabric to help hold poses but keep your muscles engaged.

USES
Supporting the shoulders in backbends, arm balances, and inversions.

BOLSTER

Having one of these is like having a huge, fluffy teddy bear around. The bolster is a great companion for restorative poses and acts as a "safety pillow" when working on transitional poses in which your head goes toward the floor.

USES
- Supporting the lower back
- Doing restorative poses
- Aiding confidence during moves

CLOTH STRAP

The traditional yoga strap is a long cloth strap with a buckle that allows it to form a small to large loop.

USES
- Lassoing the feet to help with forward folds or bending areas of limited flexibility
- Performing restorative poses
- Deepening shoulder rotation in backbends
- Supporting the shoulders in backbends, arm balances, and inversions

ONE OR TWO BLANKETS

Blankets are used similarly to bolsters, but give you more variety when it comes to width, height, and thickness.

USES
- Supporting the lower back
- Supporting a shoulder stand
- Doing abdominal work on a hardwood floor
- Performing a Savasana (typically the final pose in a sequence, where you lie flat on your back to relax and allow your body to recover)

APARIGRAHA (nongreed)
Take a walk down any main shopping strip and you'll understand this one: We are obsessed with and attached to material goods. While enjoying a good shopping spree can elevate one's mood (everyone needs a little retail therapy from time to time), be careful not to associate happiness with tangible objects. This yama seeks to keep us in the present moment instead of lusting after a wish list of unattainable goodies.

The Niyamas
Once you have a solid grip on your restraints, it's time to move on to your disciplines (niyamas), which are: saucha (cleanliness), santosa (contentment), tapas (austerity), svadhayaya (self-study), and isvara pranidhana (devotion to God).

SAUCHA (cleanliness)
Your mama probably taught you this one. While it's important to scrub behind your ears and get between your toes, this also means purity of thoughts and consumption. Take care of your body (it's your temple) by doing the physical practice, speaking your truth with compassion (there's satya!), and consuming pure, clean food.

SANTOSA (contentment)
This is the ultimate rule to truly live in the moment. We spend so much time worrying about things that may or may not ever come to be. Santosa asks that we stop planning ahead and enjoy each moment and breath as it arrives. This is tricky, but it becomes easier when you set a daily intention to be content and practice gratitude for the everyday gifts that you possess.

TAPAS (austerity)
The Sanskrit word "tap" means "to burn," so "tapas" is often referred to as "heat" or "discipline." Tapas comes from the exertion of doing the postures or being able to get out of bed when the alarm clock chimes at the crack of dawn. Practicing tapas makes us strong and enables us to show up when the going gets rough.

SVADHAYAYA (self-study)
Try saying this one three times fast! The theory here is that the better you know yourself, the more apt you are to have control over your actions, thoughts, and emotions. Svadhayaya includes things like taking the time to read this book and learn. It makes you a better citizen of the world and more mindful of your responsibilities.

ISVARA PRANIDHANA (devotion to God)
This one can get a bit sticky because the G word is used. Patanjali never cited a particular god figure in the sutras. Rather, he encouraged that we dedicate our energy and devotion toward our personal gods—Jesus, Allah, Buddha, spirit, or maybe even ourselves. It's a way to focus our meditation and realize that we're all unified and in this together.

Ready, Set, Om

Asanas

Finally! Something that we all know and love. Patanjali stressed that you must have a grip on your restraints and disciplines before you take a shot at the rigors of the physical practice. A "perfect pose" in yoga is one that you can hold with ease and stillness. During difficult poses, there should be no grunting like you do when you bench press at the gym. Your mind should become so still that all you can focus on is your body in connection to your breath. Talk about strength! My take on balance is similar. Balance isn't standing completely still—it's making peace with the fluctuations of the body and choosing to remain, regardless of the speed bumps. This is the goal of the asanas.

Pranayama

"Prana" translates as "energy" or "life force," while "ayama" means "restraint" or "control." Proficient yogis do regular pranayama practice to clear the channels of their minds in preparation for meditation. The simplicity of taking a moment out of your hectic day to breathe thoughtfully for even 1 minute can make all the difference in the world.

Pratyahara

The fifth limb is a highly useful tool for the modern-day yogi. We live in a nonstop world full of cell phones, car pools, business meetings, and jetting around. Our senses are bombarded with advertisements, videos, and constant text messages. Practicing mind withdrawal pulls us away from the external stimuli so that we can return to our thoughts. The ability to draw yourself inward lets you be aware of your surroundings without being ruled by them.

Dharana

Concentrating intently is a prerequisite for meditation. Just like a dancer chooses a single spot to gaze at to avoid falling out of a complex spin, yogis send all of their thoughts to a point in their bodies or around them. This gets you ready for the real game changer: meditation.

Dhyana

Meditation has profound effects on your stress levels and on your ultimate ability to clear your mind of the chaos of daily life. Patanjali's hope was that consistent meditation would help a yogi experience a deep connection to the universal consciousness. Put it this way: It's hard to get too angry at someone once you realize that you're mad at him because you're seeing a piece of yourself in him. This is the key to awareness, and to our next step.

Samadhi

This final step brings together all of the hard work. This is the pinnacle state of balance that we all strive to achieve. At this point, nothing throws us off, our intentions are consistently strong and pure, and our hearts and souls are full and at one with everyone else. Sign me up.

MODERN YOGA:
From Seated Poses
to Stretchy Pants

"Hatha yoga" is the umbrella term for the style of yoga Westerners practice today. When it first appeared in the 9th or 10th century, hatha yoga was a form of meditation ("finding one's comfortable seat"). "Ha" (the sun) and "tha" (the moon) is a union of two opposites. This common yogic theme suggests that practicing hatha yoga will help the practitioner unite the opposing forces of the body, mind, and soul. So, how did yogis get off their seats and start to kick asana?

In the 14th century, a Tantric sage named Swami Svatmarama wrote the *Hatha Yoga Pradipika,* the first text to describe asanas in any specific detail. It contains 16 postures addressing digestive purification, seated meditation, and energy arousal. In the late 1800s, those 16 poses evolved into 122, as set out in the first book devoted to asana, the *Sritattvanidhi*. In addition to illustrating variations on poses from the earlier hatha yoga texts, it also includes Indian wrestling exercises and gymnastics practices, many of which you may be familiar with, such as the chaturanga dandasana pushups, taught in most classes, that give you such amazing arm definition!

Vinyasa

If Patanjali was the Godfather of yoga, then Tirumalai Krishnamacharya was the hip daddy. Although he never stepped foot on American soil, Krishnamacharya is the yogi most credited with influencing the Western style of physical yoga. He saw the beauty in the physical practice and set up classes in a gymnasium in India in the 1930s. Back then, only men were invited, and they wanted the same lean physique we all crave today. K-man developed sequences that created a dynamic flow of athletic poses that we now refer to as "vinyasa yoga." Three of his most revered students in Mysore, India, were Pattabhi Jois, who founded the ashtanga system of yoga; Indra Devi, the "First Lady of Yoga" in the United States; and B. K. S. Iyengar, who created an alignment- and prop-heavy style of yoga called "Iyengar yoga."

Ready, Set, Om

The vinyasa flow ("flow" is the linking of various postures in a sequence) that we practice today is often described as linking movement with breath. It's a dynamic practice that attracts the masses because it makes you sweat, lifts your heart rate, and gives you a good workout. Vinyasa has become so mainstream that you'll find there are a plethora of options available, ranging from classes that focus on strong standing poses to sequences in which you spend most of your time on your hands or upside down. No matter how you look at it, you can expect a strong class focusing on breath and mind–body connection.

Ashtanga

Potentially one of the most rigorous yoga practices, ashtanga attracts athletes, people with strong personalities, and anyone who wants the discipline and burn ashtanga involves. Although its creator, Pattabhi Jois, passed away in 2009, his tradition continues to flourish. Ashtanga remains popular, but has an air of mystery and intimidation about it. You'll often see elite yogis practicing ashtanga because of the intense amount of dedication (and the deep postures) it requires. If you're new to ashtanga, try a led primary class—they're great intros to this amazing method without the intimidation factor.

Iyengar

Named one of the 100 most influential people in the world by *Time* magazine in 2004, B. K. S. Iyengar has made quite the splash. In the same way that Jois created a series for those in need of a vigorous workout, Iyengar created a system for the less flexible. He stressed alignment and the use of blocks to help achieve the postures. This education-intensive style has proven wildly successful and is used in teacher training across the world. Iyengar continues to teach in Pune, India.

If you've ever walked into a yoga room and been puzzled by all the odd contraptions and ropes hanging from the walls, you're probably in an Iyengar classroom. This prop-heavy style uses all sorts of creative methods and devices to help you find your best version of the pose. I highly recommend adding Iyengar to your repertoire—there is endless information to learn under the guidance of a senior Iyengar teacher.

There are many other popular styles beyond these great three: power yoga (created by Baron Baptiste and Bryan Kest), the popular heated Bikram yoga (created by Bikram Choudhury), anusara yoga (created by John Friend), kundalini yoga, and the list goes on. I teach primarily vinyasa flow, but I dabble in them all.

There is no right or wrong way to practice yoga—what makes you smile and feel good is what's right. If you try a pose or sequence you're not into, please, move on. I always tell my students that if you can't smile (or at least make a funny face), you're taking it way too seriously. The modern yogi is luckier than a kid at Baskin-Robbins: The flavors and combinations are endless, so dig in!

How Yoga Will Change Your Life

Advertisements constantly bombard us with "miracle" cures: "Eat nothing but cabbage to lose weight and feel great!" or "Take this miracle pill to shed stress and pounds." At some point we've all fallen for these empty promises—and we all know they don't work in the long run. Yet people continue to search for quick fixes to lifelong struggles—whether it's losing weight, making more money, or finding true happiness.

Yoga is genius because it can make you feel better almost instantaneously, but it also dives to the root of the problem to help you exorcize the demons of the past and move into a happy and contented present. Priceless!

Good for Your Mind

Yoga is the ultimate stress buster. It provides us with a safe place to journey to on a daily basis. The yoga mat is our own little island where we can lose cell reception, goals, and obligations and return to the simplicity of breathing, finding a connection, and being in our bodies instead of floating all around them. The breathing and meditation practice slows the pulse, eases the mind, and clears out space. Doing this daily prepares us to stay calm in even the craziest of circumstances.

We have two very distinct choices in life—love and fear. Our fear base starts when we are small children

GURUS

A sign at a yoga studio in Los Angeles proudly states in bold print, "No chanting, no granola, no gurus. YOU are your own guru." These words are accompanied by a picture of a woman who looks like she'd bite your head off before she'd encourage you to breathe through a pose. The idea of a guru—a spiritual guide—has a touch of mystery surrounding it. "Guru" is a Sanskrit word that breaks into two parts: "gu," meaning "dark," and "ru," or "light." When the two parts unite you have balance and the key to dispelling the darkness, which is enlightenment. *The Yoga Sutras* were originally written for gurus to pass on to their disciples. Today, gurus still exist, but are often referred to as "mentors" in the Western world.

My own guru was Maty Ezraty, cofounder of the prestigious Yoga-Works group of studios. This tiny, 5-foot-tall superwoman blew me away with her strength and her love. She possessed the power to make me want to practice every day! Without her guidance, I can honestly say I wouldn't be teaching today. She saw potential in me when I didn't believe in myself, and she threw my yoga tush on the fire as soon as I was out of training. I found myself teaching immediately and loving every moment of it. I had both shining and mortifying moments, like any new teacher does, but I needed her guidance to get me headed in the right direction. I think of her daily when I need inspiration or simply to say thank you in my mind. We can all benefit from this type of relationship, whether it's on a yoga mat or in our work. Be open to guidance; it helps you drop your ego and allows you to soar along the learning curve.

Ready, Set, Om

dreading the monsters that live beneath our beds and slowly evolves to affect relationships, job choices, and even coming to terms with who we are. Choosing fear is the opposite of choosing love, leaving us confused, lonely, and afraid. A study published in *BioPsychoSocial Medicine* in 2011 revealed that long-term yoga practice can significantly reduce fear, anger, and fatigue. Researchers administered the Profile of Mood States questionnaire to two groups of healthy women—one group whose members had more than 2 years of yoga experience and another group who had never practiced yoga. The long-term yoga practitioners had, on average, lower self-ratings for mental disturbance, tension-anxiety, anger-hostility, and fatigue than the control group.

When we practice yoga, we kick worry to the curb and take love, potential, and hope with us when we roll up our mats and leave a class. It's a daily reminder to set intentions for what we want instead of what we dread. Think of yoga as an open invitation to be exactly where and who you are—which is perfect. Once you lose the fear, you can soar—high.

TIP: Make a promise to yourself: When the yoga mat comes out, communication devices are turned off. Practice in a room with no phone or computer, or at least turn them off. (Putting your phone on vibrate does not count!) Dedicate this small portion of your day to yourself and no one else. Enjoy the minivacation from the grind.

Good for Your Body

"How did you get those arms? Do you lift weights?" Yogis hear this question all the time and smile knowingly as they respond, "Nope. Just yoga." Yoga's physical challenges are unique in that they require nothing but you—no weights, no machines, just the ability to lift and hold your own body weight. Along with making your physical body strong, it increases your flexibility and reshapes your attitude into one that makes you ready to win. A 2011 pilot study by the Mayo Clinic found that a comprehensive, yoga-based wellness program helped a group of employees lose weight, lower their blood pressure, increase their flexibility, decrease their body fat percentage, and improve their overall quality of life.

This kind of practice leads to a leaner, longer, more graceful body that shows strength without bulk. And in addition to a rockin' body, yoga creates endurance and confidence both physically and mentally. Now that's sexy!

Yoga not only makes you lean and foxy, but also increases your sexual desire! A 2010 study published in the *Journal of Sexual Medicine* found that yoga improves women's desire, arousal, lubrication, orgasm, and sexual satisfaction, and lessens sexual pain. So forget lingerie—shack up with your partner after sharing a yoga class! You'll bond during the mutual experience and be ready to rock.

If the gym feels like a prison, then yoga is a playground. Yoga is composed of endless creative postures, which means that you never have to do the same practice twice. There is a variation for every pose, and just when you think you've mastered a pose, someone will show you a new transition that takes it to the next level. The possibilities for growth and entertainment are endless!

TIP: Once you have settled into regularly practicing yoga (three or four times a week), here's the real test—throw out the scale! I want you to go a solid 2 weeks without looking at your weight and instead go by the way you look and feel. Worry less about the numbers. Yogis are pros at being in the present moment and unattached to results—and they're some of the hottest, fittest people around! Use your practice as a way to feel better, instead of trying to scratch digits off your weight. Trust me: It will be the best breakup ever.

Good for Your Soul

Yoga starts out as a physical practice and if we're dedicated enough, it can become a way of life. This shift in perspective can be extremely spiritual—it reminds us that we are the captains of our own ships and that we possess all the tools we need to build the best versions of ourselves. Whatever you do, keep practicing. Some days it feels amazing and on others it feels like pulling hair, but the end result after practice is always the same—feeling happy, serene, and full of soul. As Jimmy Dean said, "I can't change the direction of the wind, but I can adjust my sails to always reach my destination." Use yoga as a way to always find the silver lining—it's there! It might be hiding somewhere under your mat or stuck in your spandex, but deep breaths, solid postures, and a sense of commitment will always get you there.

TIP: The next time you find yourself confronted with a situation that makes you irritable, take a deep, cleansing breath and give yourself a minute to stop and assess. What's really going on? Are you truly listening to what's being said? Don't be so quick to react and judge. Find a sliver of positive in even the most frustrating situations. See the big picture instead of what's being shoved in your face. (And don't forget to breathe!)

WHAT'S YOUR INTENTION?

Use this section to monitor your yoga practice. Answer these questions before you begin practicing and continue to check in regularly to see how your answers evolve. Use these thoughts as guidelines for your progress, fitness, and growth.

1 I am practicing yoga because: _____

2 I am happiest when I think about: _____

3 My goal for the next month is: _____

4 My intention for the next year is: _____

5 My top two challenge poses are: _____

6 My most humbling experience on the mat was: _____

7 My fears in life are: _____

8 I love: _____

9 What makes me smile instantly is: _____

10 My favorite part of my own body is: _____

11 My top five unique gifts are: _____

12 My favorite yoga pose is: _____

13 My least favorite yoga pose is: _____

CHAPTER 2
All of Your Questions Answered

Everything you've wanted to know about yoga
(and more!)

S ay the word "yoga"

to anyone and you're sure to get a reaction. I've heard everything from, "I can't even touch my toes," to "I'm not into that granola-eating-chanting-hippie-with-armpit-hair stuff," to "Wow, can I take you on a date?"

There are plenty of opinions and mysteries surrounding the ancient practice of yoga, and I'm here to demystify them all. Whether you're looking to mellow your mind, tone your physique, boost your energy, or just try something new—or all of the above!—you'll find the answers to all of your questions here.

All of Your Questions Answered

Do I Have to Be Flexible?

Pop culture portrays yogis as Gumbys with Madonna's supertoned arms and hamstrings that never end. While eventually achieving these results isn't entirely far-fetched, you certainly don't need to have all of that to begin. Saying you're not flexible enough to do yoga is like saying you're too dirty to shower! Practicing yoga will increase your flexibility—in both your body and your mind. It takes patience, but by regularly doing a routine that caters to your target areas, even your tightest muscles will begin to relax. The key? Patience. Rome wasn't built in a day, and your hands won't fly past your knees to touch the ground in that amount of time, either. Start out slow, learn to breathe through discomfort, and you'll become limber and flexible faster than you can say "Gumby."

Will This Be a Good Workout?

Call me crazy, but I love it when a big, athletic guy walks into my advanced class wanting to give it a go. I politely suggest an intro class, and he inevitably grunts something along the lines of "Bring it, yoga chick." No problem! Within 20 minutes he's lying exhausted in a puddle of his own sweat, begging for Child's Pose.

If you're looking for an awesome aerobic workout, you're in the right place. Vinyasa flow yoga is specifically designed to build heat and keep your heart rate up throughout the class with a series of demanding standing poses, twists, and inversions. I've burned up to 400 calories during a 90-minute class! People constantly ask me if I do anything besides yoga to stay in shape.

BANDHAS

Bandhas, or "locks," are additional techniques for expanding your practice and deepening your mind–body connection. Their use certainly is not mandatory, but if you want an extra challenge, try adding these to your regular poses. I find it most useful to use the mula (base) lock when lifting your body. Try the uddiyana (center) lock when you're in Downward Facing Dog, or while lying on your back to help tone your belly.

All of these locks take some time to master, so work on them separately. Don't get frustrated if you can't feel them at first, or hold them for long. Try practicing them when you're not in poses—when you're simply seated, lying on your back, or meditating. Once you have a deeper awareness of how to engage them, invite them into your regular practice slowly, one pose at a time.

MULA (BASE) BANDHA
This is the lowest lock in the body, located between your genitals and anus. The action of locking this bandha is similar to doing a Kegel contraction. For women, it should feel as though you're holding it in while waiting for the bathroom. (Men, I've heard it described as being like walking into very cold water and having your, ahem, little buddies retract!) Engaging these muscles gives you extra energy and a sense of lightness and lift that you can use to float through your practice. (Not to mention a little extra spice in the sack!) Just be careful not to overengage: You should be able to squeeze these inner muscles without anyone noticing.

UDDIYANA (CENTER) BANDHA
This bandha lives in your belly. To perform it, exhale until you've emptied your core breath and then draw your navel toward your spine. It should feel like someone has taken a vacuum cleaner to your lower abdomen and is shifting the contents up into your rib cage for storage. This bandha is excellent for toning and cleansing your core, as well as for enhancing stability. Engaging these muscles helps to build fire (which burns fat!) and ease built-up tension.

JALANDHARA (THROAT) BANDHA
The last and highest lock is the connection between your chin and chest. Lift your chest up as you drop your chin down to create this lock, which helps to prevent energy from escaping the upper body. This is most useful when you're working on pranayama (breath control).

I take long walks, hike, and dabble in Pilates to complement my yoga practice. But I certainly don't need to spend any extra hours in the gym. You'll kiss the gym good-bye once you catch the yoga bug. It burns calories and fat, lengthens and tones your muscles, and—most importantly—it's mentally engaging, stress busting, and flat-out fun.

Will I Have to Do Weird Chanting? What Is 'Om'?

Chanting is traditionally part of a yoga practice, but by no means is it required or even included in many classes. Chants are often made up of "mantras," which are words or groups of words meant to aid in meditation and transformation. Some teachers will sing or chant at the beginning or end of class, or both. "Om," which means, "the sound of the universe," is voiced as a way to join all of the practitioners together. Usually "om" is chanted three times—the teacher begins and the class members join in.

It may feel silly at first, but chanting "om" is a great way to tune out the chatter in your head and focus your energy on something simple. Of course, you can always opt to just sit quietly instead. Yoga is not about judgment or competition and should never make you feel uncomfortable. Whether you jive to the chanting or not, remember that it's just a small part of yoga practice that you can adapt to fit your own needs. Keep an open mind. Sometimes you'll want just a physical workout, and sometimes a little "om" goes a long way.

What Does 'Namaste' Mean? Why Do People Say It Holding Their Hands as If Praying?

"Namaste," a commonly used salutation in India, roughly translates to "the divinity in me respects and bows to the divinity in you." It takes the whole concept of, "I see you" from James Cameron's blockbuster hit *Avatar* to an even deeper level. The joining of the hands in front of the heart is called "anjali mudra" and is meant to symbolize respect and union (the connection of the palms). This does not have anything to do with the hand position for prayer that you use in church. Rather, it is an Indian salutation that has survived for thousands of years. It does not disrespect religion by any means—it is a symbol of respect. Overall, it's just a really beautiful way to greet or say good-bye to someone. On that note, namaste!

Is Yoga Religious?

Yoga is a spiritual practice, but that should not be confused with religious practice. It is designed to connect the body, breath, spirit, and mind. Yoga has no formal creed or services to attend. It exists to unify our minds and bodies. Yoga originated in India, so it is often associated with the Hindu religion. You may see representations of deities such as Shiva, Hanuman, and Ganesha in some yoga studios, but they're not there to be worshipped. They simply represent stories and lessons of the past and an energetic way of living. Ganesha, for example, is "the destroyer of obstacles." Some teachers will mention him when they're guiding students through challenging postures. Many studios will show no Indian influence at all.

Remember: Yoga is a practice, not worship. Whether you include a deeper spiritual aspect is up to you. The poses and sequences in this book have been designed to improve your shape, clear your mind, and give you the energy to be your best self ever!

Do You Need to Be Vegan or Vegetarian to Practice Yoga?

In a word, no. But this is a huge debate within the yoga community. One of the rules in yoga is ahimsa (nonviolence). This can be interpreted in many ways and is often cited as a reason to not eat meat. The *Hatha Yoga Pradipika,* one of hatha yoga's oldest texts, states in a passage describing proper yoga practice: "Food injurious to a yogi: bitter, sour, saltish, hot, ... intoxicating liquors, fish, meat, ... etc., should not be eaten."

Let's put it this way: Your yoga practice is going to feel pretty heavy if you scarf down a T-bone steak right before you hit the mat. There are definitely health benefits to eating a primarily vegetarian diet and staying away from processed foods. However, if you're a meat lover, there's no reason

your diet should come into conflict with your yoga practice. There are more ways than ever to eat consciously—locally sourced, organic meats from grass-fed, humanely raised animals are available in most grocery stores. I love my diet of fresh vegetables, quinoa, fruits, and fish, with the occasional meat dish. I recommend fueling your body with a diet that's as healthy and natural as possible, whether you eat meat or not.

How Often Do I Need to Practice to See Results?

Depending on your specific goals, there is a wide spectrum of answers to this one. My advice: Listen to your body. Yoga can be practiced safely every day. For total newbies who want to jump-start their practice, I recommend sessions of anywhere from 20 to 90 minutes long on 3 or 4 days a week. Stick to a routine in the beginning so you'll become disciplined, and focus on a small group of postures so you can measure your results. Your yoga practice will constantly evolve—the goal shouldn't be to "perfect" a posture and then move on. You'll feel a great sense of accomplishment from simply being able to reach closer to your toes than ever before, as well as on the day you do your first headstand!

It's important to look at your results in the grand scheme of things to keep from feeling disappointed. Everyone has bad days when they just can't concentrate or don't have as much energy as they'd like. Your progress will be evident over time, so don't worry about what happens day-to-day. Set goals and then, like in any other sport, practice! Choose two or three postures and make them a regular focus. This consistency will help you better understand your body's progress. To quote Pattabhi Jois, "Yoga is 99 percent practice, 1 percent theory. Practice, and all is coming."

Will I Lose Weight?

Absolutely! A regular yoga practice combined with a healthy diet is guaranteed to transform your body. Whether you want to lose 5, 10, 15 pounds—or even more—yoga is a fabulous way to burn calories, tone muscles, and create a lean, sexy shape. The best fat-blasting yoga styles are vinyasa and power flow, because they build a great amount of heat by focusing on strong holds and challenging postures aimed at burning calories. Not only that, the combination of stretching and strength building also creates that long, lean physique that yogis are famous for.

Of course, you can do all the yoga you want and not see a difference if you're eating poorly. Chapter 4 has all the healthy eating tips you need to complement your work on the mat.

Should I Practice When I'm Menstruating?

I lovingly refer to menstruation as the "ladies' holiday." This often-uncomfortable time of the month is your body's way of cleaning house, and it should be treated with respect. The first few days

MANTRAS AND CHANTING

A mantra is a word or phrase that is repeated over and over again. The original meaning of the word is "the creative projection of the mind through sound." "Man" symbolizes the mind, while "tra" means "wave" or "projection."

Our bodies are full of energy, waves, and vibrations. Naad yoga (the yoga of sound) is based on how sound vibrations affect the body, mind, and spirit. There are 84 meridian points on just the roofs of our mouths alone, and as you chant, the movements of your tongue touch certain meridian points and cause changes in the chemistry of your brain that evoke a particular energetic state your desire—it lifts you up when you need energy and soothes when you need calm.

Santa Monica–based kundalini teacher Kia Miller explains: "All thoughts are carried along vibration frequencies, or waves. Certain thoughts have a particular kind of vibration, which defines how we feel and what we project onto others. Chanting mantras, either silently or out loud, is a way of consciously directing your mind, ultimately creating a sense of mental calm and peace. Ancient mantras are considered codes (think of a yogic Sherlock Holmes) that unlock and harmonize our energy. Different mantras evoke different energetic states, but ultimately all lead us to a deeper connection with ourselves. Mantras encourage a place where we transcend the chatter of the mind and tune in to our infinite power."

Here are some simple mantras to try.

OM
I know you've heard this one, but it's an easy place to start. "Om" translates to "the sound of the universe." It's a great way to ground yourself and connect to your surroundings.

SO HUM
This is another common mantra used in meditation. It translates to "I am" and "that is."

SAT NAM
"Truth is my identity."

ONG SO HUNG
"What I am to be, I already am."

BRAHMARI
This is actually just a sound like a buzzing bee makes. You should feel your lips and mouth vibrate as you hum.

LOKA SAMASTA SUKHINO BHAVANTU
I know this one is a mouthful, but its message is beautiful. It roughly means "May all beings everywhere be happy and free and may the thoughts, words, and actions of my own life contribute in some way to that happiness and to that freedom for all."

of a period can be intense physically. But movement can offer relief from menstrual cramps, and many gentle yoga postures such as Legs Up the Wall (see page 145) also can help.

There are differing opinions on whether you should invert—be upside down—during your period. Many people claim the bloodflow will "get stuck" if you are upside down or that there are physical contraindications to inverting. The menstrual cycle is a sacred part of being a woman, and when something is trying to come out, it doesn't make a whole lot of sense to flip around and make it flow upside down. I do recommend skipping inversions for the first few days and practicing short holds toward the end of menstruation. But nothing will "get stuck", and if it feels good to kick your feet up, go for it!

As far as a full practice goes, it's completely up to you based on how you feel. Let your body take its natural course and do a gentle practice if need be. Enjoy your holiday, relax, and have a piece of chocolate. You'll be back to a full practice in just a day or two.

Will Yoga Practice Help Reduce Stress? How Do I Breathe?

If I could bottle the amount of stress relief that yoga provides, it would sell faster than the Missoni collection did at Target! Yoga is an amazing physical workout that has the huge added benefit of stress relief.

A large part of this relief comes from simply breathing. Pranayama (breath control) is used in all postures. "Ujjayi breath" is performed by inhaling and exhaling through the nostrils with the mouth softly closed. This method of breathing is what allows you to focus when your mind starts to race or a posture becomes challenging. The combination of focusing on both the breath and the posture is the secret to yoga's amazing ability to eliminate stress. It's what helps to clear the chatter in your head and transport you to a calm and centered state of mind. Whether you practice in a class or in your own home, yoga creates a refuge where you can escape from the chaos of everyday life. It's a physical and mental activity that reconnects you with yourself, as opposed to concentrating on what everyone else demands of you. And even if you don't have time for a full practice, taking just 5 minutes to stop and breathe can have a dramatic effect on the rest of your day. Your pulse slows, your mind softens, and you're ready to move forward stress free.

TRY THIS: Find a quiet, comfortable space where you can tune out the day and be by yourself. Sit cross-legged comfortably with your spine lifted straight and tall. Close your eyes. Inhale slowly for a count of 4. Hold your breath for 4, and then slowly exhale for a count of 4. Repeat this sequence for 1 to 5 minutes. Open your eyes. You'll be amazed by how relaxed you feel. All it takes is 5 minutes a day to make a big difference!

What Should I Eat before Practice?

Yoga is full of movement—deep twists, hops, transitions, and inversions. I recommend that you not eat or drink (much) for 2 hours before you practice so you can hit the mat on a relatively empty stomach. If you practice first thing in the morning and feel sick without any food, eat something light, like a protein bar or some almond butter on toast. Otherwise, stick to the 2-hour rule. Remember to drink plenty of water afterward and to wait for about an hour before you sit down for a full meal.

What Should I Wear?

Cute yoga pants have become weekend wardrobe staples, but they do make a difference on the mat. Most dynamic styles of yoga require fitted clothes, since there's lots of movement. You want something that will move with you and not get in your way. Look for tights or straight-leg yoga pants made with spandex. There are plenty of options for tops as well, many of them with built-in bras and support. A fitted T-shirt works well, too, if you're not comfortable with baring much skin. Definitely avoid baggy shirts! They'll fall over your face in poses like Downward Facing Dog and inversions.

For more restorative (or "yin") practice, you can opt for soft, nonconstricting clothes that don't need to be quite as fitted.

GREAT BRANDS TO CHECK OUT:

Lululemon: This Canadian company has taken the States by storm with its flattering bottoms and whimsical colors. Somehow, its yoga pants make everyone's behind look amazing.

Hard Tail Forever: This California company's line is carried by department stores and comes in every color and pattern imaginable.

Beyond Yoga: This company offers a more sophisticated line that concentrates on elegant shapes and fantastic fabrics.

Gap, Old Navy, and Target also offer yoga gear that's affordable and super comfy.

Once you have your outfit, you'll need to get a yoga mat, blocks, and a strap. (See "More Yoga Resources" on page 391 for great Web sites that carry these, as well as "What You'll Need" on page 4.)

TIP: The one thing you should never have with you during your practice: your phone. A ringing, vibrating, beeping, or blinking phone or laptop pulls you out of your focus and makes it impossible to practice fully. You will survive without your phone! I promise. Take the time to disconnect from your agenda—whether it's for 15 minutes or even a full hour—and you will reap the benefits of reconnecting with yourself.

All of Your Questions Answered

AIM TRUE

"Aim true" is my motto. For me, it means that I start each and every day with a clear intention to be true to who I am, who I want to continue to be, and what makes my heart beat strong! I love the expression "aim true" because it's extremely personal and translates into something different for each person who uses it. Take a look through the principles I've outlined here, and think about how you can use them in your practice and your life. When we aim true, we will always hit our mark—and yoga helps us do just that.

ASANA

Nothing says ahhhh like a beautifully executed yoga posture, also known as an asana (Sanskrit for "posture"). There is beauty in the postures themselves, not to mention the attractive physique that comes from a dedicated practice! Asanas also offer mental clarity and stress relief. No matter how cranky, tired, or sore you feel, I guarantee you'll be refreshed and renewed after a yoga session. Connecting your breath with the poses is like an instant hit of relaxation, and the sequence of postures strengthens and detoxes your body. Asanas pack a double whammy of physical and mental power.

INTENTION

Professional and elite athletes often refer to "the zone." It's a state of mind in which their focus and their intentions are completely present in that moment. Whether they're about to throw the perfect fastball or stride across the finish line in record time, athletes use the zone to hone and sharpen their training. In yoga, the zone is simply "intention." At the beginning of every practice, take a moment to set your intention, whether it's a specific goal ("I want to shake off the fight I just had with my boyfriend") or a more universal ideal ("I want to cultivate a stronger body and attitude"). The cool thing about yoga is that it reminds us to set an intention every time we unroll our mats. An intention sharpens our ability to be mindful and aware. Talk about multitasking: Yoga helps you shape your body, relieve stress, and become a more compassionate person.

TRY THIS: Write down your intention every morning for an entire week. Make note of when you waiver from your intention throughout the day and do your best to keep it pumping strong regardless of the scenario. Remember how it felt to connect with your intention during your practice. Know that no matter how tough times get, you still have that in you somewhere and can tap into that reserve whenever you need it.

MANIFESTATION

"I'm in charge of my own happiness, so you're off the hook." This is one of my favorite quotes from Abraham Hicks, and it makes me smile every time I see it. By nature, we often believe that happiness will come from something external—a higher-paying job, a wedding ring, or that dream car. We spend so much energy focusing on what we lack that we forget all the powerful stuff we already possess! Yoga reminds us about how much powerful potential we have within ourselves. We just need to remember it's there and learn how to use it.

Maybe you've never done an arm balance or balanced upside down on your head. In fact, maybe you've never tried Downward Dog. But you're here! You've opened this book and you kept reading it. See yourself doing the pose. Once you can see yourself doing it, imagine what it feels like. Start to practice the pose in your mind and then invite it into your reality. It might sound like a joke, but manifesting is powerful stuff. (Anyone who's ever read Rhonda Byrne's *The Secret* will know exactly what I'm talking about!) Slowly, your body begins to change. Now you're practicing a half headstand without breaking a sweat. Next thing you know, you're balancing against a wall and then effortlessly floating into a headstand in the middle of the room. I'm serious! This is manifestation. Claim what you want, and you'll have it.

TRY THIS: Keep a yoga journal. Pick two or three " challenge poses" that inspire and maybe even scare you. Figure out what makes you fearful (e.g., "I'm worried about hurting my shoulder" or "I'm afraid of falling") and write that down. Record what works, what doesn't, and take a look back at your progress once you nail the pose. Remember that mistakes can teach us so much, and a good sense of humor goes a long way! Enjoy the journey. (Note: If you do have an injury, speak to your doctor or physical therapist about whether you should do certain poses, or if they should be modified to suit your needs.)

THANKFULNESS

Gratitude is woven throughout yoga. Teachers consistently remind their students to be thankful—for being able to come to practice and to twist and turn their bodies. Yoga nurtures flexibility along with strength, allowing us to do simple things like touching our toes or opening our chests into a backbend—things that many people cannot do. These movements feel good physically, but they also make us feel good about our physical abilities.

This practice of gratitude makes us truly understand how to respect others, too. It can start simply: Look flight attendants in the eye and thank them genuinely for their help. It might just make their day after dealing with a bunch of grumpy passengers! Tell your significant other how attractive he or she is. Call up your mom and say, "Thanks, Mom. You rock and I really love you." Of course, the world will immediately want in on the secret to your happiness—so share what you've learned! Use yoga to build your own gratitude and encourage others to do the same.

RELAXATION

Our world is constantly surging forward and sometimes it feels like our heads are spinning. Our overworked minds and bodies can only handle so much before breaking down or collapsing entirely. Whether you take a few minutes to focus on your breath or perform an entire restorative sequence, yoga can help you truly chill out. Ujjayi breathing, or victorious breath (see page 25), acts like a steamer for our brains, ironing out excessive wrinkles and bumps that keep us from seeing clearly. Restorative postures are also used to release your hips, lower back, hamstrings, and chest, and to put you completely at ease. Your body will be so calm that your mind will want to join t he party! Remember, start by stopping. Take a breath. Let go.

TRY THIS: Pile two pillows or place a bolster next to a wall right before bedtime. Practice the Legs Up the Wall pose (see page 145) for 5 to 10 minutes. Cover your eyes with a towel or eye pillow. Take long, slow breaths and use only the sound of it to drown out any thoughts. When you're done, keep your mind quiet (avoid using the computer or other electronics and interacting with others) and crawl straight into bed for a sound sleep.

UNITY

The actual translation of "yoga" is "yoke," which is exactly what it does: Yoga unifies the body, mind, and spirit. There are few physical activities that can boast such a résumé. Yoga seamlessly weaves this powerful trio together to give us the ultimate gift—contentment. Contentment (or "santosha" in Sanskrit) is the ability to achieve flow on our yoga mats and in the rest of our lives. Standing on one foot isn't difficult when you know it's okay to lower the raised one and try again. Similarly, that hurtful co-worker won't leave a scratch if you know you've done your best. When we unify our bodies, minds, and spirits with yoga, grace and confidence follow, and doors open up all around us.

ENJOYMENT

I'm just going to let the cat out of the bag: Yoga is supposed to be fun! Yoga has been portrayed for years as a dedicated and quiet discipline that should be practiced in isolation and seriousness. I'm here to tell you the complete opposite. A regular yoga practice will make starting each day with a dance party on your bed seem totally normal. Why not?

I was that yogi in the ashtanga room who always got scolded for talking too much or laughing. The funny thing is, I never changed. I kept laughing when I felt compelled to stop (which was quite often, because I was falling all over myself). I'm so grateful that I never gave up that energy and passion, because it turned me into the teacher I am today—one who's loving, compassionate, and funny. I've learned how to make the practice accessible through humor and have reached many students through my teaching. I always remind my students when they're doing poses: If you can't smile or at least make a funny face, you're taking it way too seriously. There are enough obstacles in life that will make you pause and grimace; yoga doesn't have to be one of them! Use yoga as a tool to find the silver lining in everything and laughter and beauty in everything you do. Embrace and enjoy your life!

CHAPTER 3

From Om to Tone

How yoga gets you fit

"You're so strong.

What else do you do besides yoga?"

If only I had a dollar for every time I've heard that! There is a general conception that yoga will make you flexible, limber, and lean, but it can't possibly help you maintain your overall fitness as well as other types of workouts do. I'm here to prove otherwise! Let's start by taking a look at what "fitness" means.

Merriam-Webster's Collegiate Dictionary defines "fit" as "sound physically and mentally." Sounds like the results of yoga to me! The American College of Sports Medicine identifies three different types of fitness that are key to maintaining good health: cardiovascular, muscle strength and tone, and flexibility.

How Yoga Gets You Fit

Cardiovascular

This is the style of fitness that most people think of first, and it's what you get from doing heart-pumping, heavy-breathing, fast-moving actions. Cardiovascular exercise works your heart, lungs, and blood vessels, increasing stamina and decreasing your risk for heart disease and maybe some types of cancer.

Whether you can achieve a great cardio session with yoga depends on the type of yoga practiced. Vinyasa and power yoga create constant movement that fires up your body, gets the sweat pouring, and delivers a heart-thumping good time! The "flow" element and the challenging long holds in standing, balancing, and twisting postures that are common to these styles of yoga increase your heart rate.

Another huge element of cardiovascular health is how well you can breathe. Moving without fatigue depends on maximal oxygen uptake—in other words, how well oxygen enters your lungs. The fitter you are, the better you transport oxygen. The entire yoga practice—no matter what style you practice—revolves around connecting movement with breath. Ujjayi breath (see "Victorious Breath" on page 25) involves inhaling and exhaling through the nostrils with the mouth softly closed. The goal is to keep the breath fluid and calm—whether it's during seated meditation or 10 sun salutations into your session. The more you practice yoga, the better your breath control becomes, which ultimately improves your cardiovascular health.

Prominent yoga teacher John Schumacher performed a study at the age of 52 to prove that yoga does indeed make you fit. Schumacher underwent physiological testing at a lab in Gaithersburg, Maryland, while he performed a variety of fitness tests that measured heart and exercise recovery rates. His doctor told him he had less than a 1 percent chance of suffering a cardiac event. This from a man whose only form of physical activity was yoga and breathwork!

POSES TO TRY:
Sun Salutation (see page 44)
Warrior II (see page 72)
Warrior III (see page 74)
Handstand (see page 116)
Boat (see page 139)
Revolved Chair (see page 89)

Muscular Strength and Tone

This refers to the actual strength and endurance of your muscles. Doctors agree that as we age, we lose muscle mass as well as bone density. It's part of life, but yoga is a great counteractive tool. It not only helps to build muscular strength with the repetition of postures, but it is also a load-bearing exercise that increases bone density. Plus, every pound of muscle you have burns between 25 and 50 calories a day without you even unrolling your mat, so don't be afraid to eat your spinach and practice your chaturangas!

One major appeal of yoga is that you don't need dumbbells, gym machines, or any other fancy equipment to achieve awesome muscle tone—you just need a nonskid surface. Practicing yoga is like driving a car with a manual transmission—you understand and control your vehicle better. You don't need a machine to make the shifting decisions for you because yoga teaches you how to align your body and mind. Now that's strong.

POSES TO TRY:
  Pushup (see page 143)
  Plank (see page 141)
  Chair (see page 53)
  Goddess (see page 157)
  Handstand (see page 116)

Flexibility

It wouldn't take a lawyer to prove that yoga makes you limber. Yoga clearly improves flexibility in our bodies as well as in our perspectives. In a British study from researchers at the University of York, people—primarily middle-age women—reported that they had improved back function and flexibility after doing 12 weeks of yoga, compared with those receiving regular care from the British National Health Service. As we age, our bodies grow tighter and shorter.

This lessening of mobility is one of the major causes of chronic pain and injury. Lower-back pain is often caused by tight hip flexors or hamstring muscles putting tension on the lower back. The rounded, heavy shoulders resulting from poor posture fatigue the neck muscles and tighten the jaw. (Anyone who works long hours at a desk will know exactly what I'm talking about!) A regular yoga practice strengthens and elongates the muscles, allowing for a balanced existence.

Yoga is the ultimate fitness routine because it builds cardio strength with flow; develops muscular tone with long, strong holds; and creates flexibility with almost every pose. It's also completely customizable: You can dive into power and vinyasa classes to kick-start your heart rate and sweat like you're in a sauna. Or look to Iyengar yoga for intense holds. Try a yin practice, which focuses on opening and releasing tension with long holds in restorative postures. There's something for everyone at every level.

Will yoga make you fit? You bet. And that's not all.

VICTORIOUS BREATH

Ujjayi breath: Start by stopping. Slow down your breath. Begin to transfer from regular breathing to breathing in and out through your nostrils with your lips softly closed. You'll feel a slight rush like a wave at the back of your throat, but don't do anything that feels forced. The breath should be even, relaxed, and smooth.

Yoga and Weight Loss

Anyone who's lost weight on a diet only to regain it knows that the world of weight loss is almost as frustrating as watching edited reruns of *Sex and the City*.

Why is it so tough to get rid of that stubborn muffin top, or even those last 5 pounds? Before you ask the blanket question, "Why can't I lose weight?" consider what else is happening in your life. Are you stressed out from work?

How Yoga Gets You Fit

Too busy to get to the gym? Constantly reaching for comfort foods instead of healthy options (and then feeling guilty about it)? We've all been there. But you don't have to ride this diet roller coaster forever. Once again, yoga comes to the rescue!

A 2005 study done by the National Cancer Institute looked at two groups of 15,500 healthy middle-age men and women. Over the same period of time, those who practiced yoga lost about 5 pounds, while those who didn't practice gained 14 pounds.

A regular yoga practice can help you evaluate the source of the imbalance that might be at the root of your weight problem. As you get more comfortable with aligning your mind and body, you'll feel calm and centered—and you'll find it easier than ever to make positive, healthy choices and to shed any extra pounds for good. In addition to a new mind-set, yoga also offers a host of physical benefits that help you lose weight: It relaxes muscles that are tight from inactivity, tension, and stress. It builds muscle strength, increases your range of motion, and can be a great cardio workout, as well.

All styles of yoga lengthen, tone, and strengthen your muscles, but you gotta burn calories in order to lose weight! A vinyasa-style practice—in which movement and breath are linked in the postures—builds a lot of heat, which burns a lot of calories. Ashtanga and power yoga deliver similar results, but take care, because these styles are intense and may prove too daunting for a beginner, possibly ruining your yoga experience altogether.

No matter whether you're a beginner or a more advanced practitioner, start slow. Make sure you understand the postures before you throw yourself into a whirlwind of movements and unfamiliar stances. This approach

REAL-LIFE WEIGHT LOSS WITH YOGA

I'm just over 5 feet tall and weighed about 115 pounds when I became pregnant. The first trimester was a bit of a nightmare because I had hyperemesis, which is chronic morning sickness, 24/7, for 3 months. To avoid becoming extremely ill I had to eat every 2 hours, and I was unable to do much because I was so nauseated. I spent the majority of the time lying down.

The rest of the pregnancy was wonderful—except that I consistently gained 7 to 10 pounds between doctor's appointments. At full-term, I weighed 174 pounds! I secretly hoped I would have a 50-pound baby. Every extra pound felt heavy and sluggish on my body and my mind.

On March 13, 2010, I gave birth to a beautiful, healthy baby girl. I had taken some yoga classes in the past, and the deep breathing helped me immensely during delivery. At my postnatal checkup with my midwife, I weighed in at 154 pounds. That was rough. I tried to stay positive, and everyone told me that with breastfeeding, I would lose the weight.

Well, I didn't! Over the next 9 months I lost only 4 pounds.

I was sick of being so negative toward myself. I made a New Year's resolution to start eating differently and to do yoga.

I began practicing three or four times a week with videos and a class, and slowly but surely I started losing weight. I loved that I could practice in my own home. After we celebrated my daughter's first birthday, I noticed a big difference in my weight when I saw the pictures from her party. I looked great, but more importantly, I felt great. Not only were the inches gone, but also my aches and pains from carrying the extra weight on my petite frame had disappeared. To date, I have lost almost 40 pounds! Yoga changed my life, my body, and my self-esteem. Mostly, it has allowed me to become the energetic mom that I'm supposed to be. I'm so proud that I feel like someone my daughter can look up to.

—*Laura Helms, 28, of Portland, Oregon*

follows the principle of ahimsa—nonviolence to the body. The best way to lose weight and get in shape is by making sensible and loving choices for your body, step by step. Think of it this way: If you threw yourself cannonball-style into a swimming pool without learning to swim first, you'd quickly realize that wearing those dorky floats was a good idea after all! Swallow your pride and remember that anything worth having takes time.

The Stress Factor

One of the biggest factors in weight gain is, plain and simple, stress. The basic science is that stress releases cortisol, a hormone secreted by the adrenal glands. When your stress level is normal, cortisol aids in glucose metabolism; regulates blood pressure; and maintains blood sugar, immune function, and the inflammatory response, which is the "fight-or-flight" response to a perceived threat. However, when your body chronically experiences a high level of stress, cortisol secretion kicks into high gear and suppresses thyroid function, decreases bone density and muscle mass over time, and lowers immunity. Worst of all, it increases abdominal fat. Yup, you heard me—stress creates belly fat.

Cortisol stimulates fat and carbohydrate metabolism, which increases your appetite. Chronic stress can lead to chronically elevated cortisol levels, leaving you with a bigger appetite and the need to work out harder to burn off what you ate. Researchers have also shown that cortisol tends to deposit more fat in the abdominal area than anywhere else. Studies of women with excess fat in their abdomens showed that they had higher cortisol levels and more stressful lifestyles than women whose fat was stored in their hips.

Now, before you get stressed-out about being stressed-out, stop and breathe! Take a minute to ask yourself: Where is this stress coming from, and how is it affecting my behavior? A stressful lifestyle can lead to many unhealthy habits, not the least of which are binge eating, smoking, drinking, and grabbing junk food instead of a healthy meal. These are all crutches that you can and should replace with the best support system of all—yoga!

Yoga should be called the bad-habit buster. Many unhealthy habits nurtured by stress find the nearest exit after even just a few weeks of practicing. According to a 2011 study, British university workers reported an improvement in well-being and resilience to stress after participating in six hour-long yoga classes over the course of 6 weeks. The participants in the yoga group also scored higher on clear-mindedness, energy, and confidence than those who did not practice yoga. The calming, meditative effects of yoga help you relax, focus, and control your stress. So take a deep breath, unroll your mat (even just for 15 minutes), and get ready to let stress go and invite health in.

CHAPTER 4

The Art of Mindful Eating

Let yoga play a starring role in nourishing yourself

I used to practice yoga

in one of the most prestigious classes in Los Angeles, surrounded by cream-of-the-crop yogis. These men and women were of all shapes and sizes, but had two traits in common—they were beautiful and they moved with the grace of Baryshnikov. Their lean muscles cut through the air flawlessly. I was in awe. I recall a practitioner telling me that my fresh-out-of-college body would change before my very eyes—and a mere 6 months later it had! I dropped 2 inches off my waist, I could see muscles I never knew I possessed, and my endurance grew by the minute.

The Art of Mindful Eating

While these physical changes were no doubt welcome results of all my yoga practice, they were also due to a shift in my diet. I was still enjoying my favorite foods from college: pasta, mac 'n' cheese, veggies with cream cheese, Mexican takeout, and so on. But as my practice had deepened, I had noticed changes in my cravings. Suddenly, I wanted fresh fruits, dark greens, smoothies, and lighter fare. And I noticed how awful my practice could be after a crazy, indulgent night out at a restaurant or downing a pint of Ben & Jerry's.

As I continued to practice yoga, I started to listen to what my body was really saying: I learned to distinguish "I'm hungry" from "I'm dehydrated" and to pay attention when I felt I was lacking a certain nutrient. I also started to gauge how full I was truly feeling, instead of looking at a menu with big saucer eyes and gobbling up whatever was put in front of me.

In a study published in the *Journal of the American Dietetic Association,* a group of mostly female participants were given a mindful eating questionnaire (MEQ). Researchers found that yoga was associated with a higher MEQ score, whereas walking and moderate or intense physical activity were not. The ultimate goal is to find an active routine that fits your body and schedule and complement it with a thoughtful and nutritious diet. Yoga has the special ability to blend the best of both worlds. In Chapter 3 we discussed how yoga keeps you fit with physical postures. Yoga also reduces your stress level, allowing you to make more balanced and intelligent choices when it comes to your plate. Let's take a look at how yoga can curb your appetite and reprogram your taste buds into making smart choices.

To Eat or Not to Eat— Before a Yoga Class

The most common advice is to not eat or drink anything for 2 hours before you practice. It's similar to the advice about not eating before swimming: You don't want to cramp up at the bottom of the pool, or your mat. A full stomach can be uncomfortable enough on its own, but add in deep twists, inversions, and backbends, and you've got some serious indigestion on your hands! Trust me, you don't want to be that person in class who's holding back gas or making gurgling sounds that make your neighbors nervous. Big meals slow you down. They decrease your energy level and stamina for constant (and deep) movement.

If you find yourself light-headed from hunger before yoga or you like to practice first thing in the morning, stick to light snacks: fruits, almond butter, tea, or even a small container of yogurt. Save the full meal for after class, but don't dive right in: Eating a large amount of food immediately after practice often causes nausea. Allow your body to cool down first. Drink plenty of water, take a shower, then sit down for a nice meal. Your body will thank you.

The same 2-hour rule also goes for liquids. If your belly is full of liquid you'll feel a whole lot of sloshing going on, and frequent trips to the restroom will disrupt the flow of your practice (or worse, all your classmates' flow, too). I don't recommend drinking water during your practice, either. This might come as a blow if you're used to lugging your water bottle everywhere, but there is a reason for this advice. One of the main objectives of yoga is to build heat in the body. This heat, or discipline, helps you burn through mental distractions *and* calories. Water puts out the fire, so instead of reaching for the bottle, let the heat rise! More sweating means more detoxing is taking place, which leads to my next subject.

Alcohol and Yoga

All work and no play makes us dull yogis, and there's nothing wrong with having a fun night out on the town. Just know that you will smell like that margarita the next day as you sweat out all the toxins. The first 20 minutes of yoga when you have a hangover may feel like the worst minutes of your life, but be strong! Once you get past the pain, the sweat will come, the twists will wring you out, and you'll be clear and clean by the end. Check out my yoga for hangovers sequence on page 224 for a foolproof way to feel more like yourself on a Sunday morning.

In addition to helping you detox from a great party, yoga can also encourage you to cut back to a healthy level of alcohol consumption. Once you maintain a regular practice, you'll find yourself wanting to show up to practice in the best form possible. Staying up late and drinking excessively won't seem as alluring because they will interfere with your ability to hold the more challenging poses. Think of these yoga postures as loving chaperones, guiding us in the right direction.

The Carnivore's Dilemma

Hardcore yogis tend to be vegans or vegetarians because they practice the rule of ahimsa, which means "nonviolence." The interpretation is broad, but many people view it as a reason not to kill or consume animals and/or their by-products. I'm a strong believer that we should eat what makes our bodies feel best, but there is a yogic spin to everything, and eating is no exception. If you've never explored a vegetarian diet and are curious, there's no better time than the present. Yoga's emphasis on movement may lessen your desire for heavy foods like red meat. (Conversely, it could make you crave it even more!) Join in the "Meatless Mondays" craze as a way to cut back, and see how your body responds. There are tons of recipes and ideas available at Womenshealthmag. com for you to try!

At the end of the day, do what makes your body run best, but make good decisions. It's all about being conscious. Whether you're chowing down on a big salad or a thick steak, know where your food comes from and how it affects your body and the greater world around you.

The Art of Mindful Eating

Conscious Eating

Eating is one of those activities that the brain easily shuts down for. The rules are simple: Open mouth, insert food. Chew. Swallow. Repeat. While many of us eat mindlessly as an emotional fix, we can also fall into a "food coma" regarding the food itself, where it comes from, and what's in it. But avoiding this is especially important when it comes to consuming meat. The majority of American meat comes from large factories, not small farms. These factories often keep their animals in unnatural conditions, where they are confined in close quarters and fed fillers and fatteners such as corn— along with the antibiotics, vitamin supplements, and growth hormones needed to make them healthy in such conditions. Buying from these meat sources supports this system.

Concentrating a large number of animals in a relatively small space is also environmentally unsound. Animal agriculture produces a great deal of air and water pollution and causes 80 percent of the world's deforestation annually, as forests and jungles are razed to establish new feedlots. Producing, transporting, processing, and marketing foods from factory farms rely heavily on fossil fuels, which are rapidly being depleted and which contribute to climate change. In a nutshell, mainstream animal agriculture is definitely not the way to go. So what can you do? Let's look at three easy ways to buy meat in an eco-friendly manner.

GO ORGANIC

Buy meats from animals that were raised free of antibiotics, added hormones, GMOs, and other drugs.

Organically raised animals are not given any drugs for reasons other than illness, and they're not fed genetically modified feed, nor can their own genes be modified. They are raised in much healthier environments and are fed organic food rather than something from a laboratory test tube. Check the packaging to make sure it says USDA organic.

SUPPORT MORE HUMANE, ETHICAL TREATMENT OF ANIMALS

Factory farming is not a pretty sight. Animals are treated solely as products and live their entire lives confined to small cages or overcrowded pens. Look for products labeled "free range," "cage free," and "grass fed." They may cost a few more dollars at the grocery store, but that money goes toward both a cruelty-free way of eating and your overall health.

BUY LOCAL

You'll lighten your carbon footprint by purchasing meats from a local farm. The closer the farm, the less distance the products need to travel, which ultimately means less fossil fuel consumption. Small farms and family farms also tend to have cows, chickens, and other livestock that serve multiple purposes, not just providing food. When you purchase local products at your grocery store or farmer's market, you'll know that the money is going back into a community business, not a multinational food conglomerate. So choose local, organic animal products whenever you can. It's better for your health, your local community, and the larger community as a whole.

A Fresh Start

Whether you're meat loving, veggie, or vegan, there's more information than ever available to help you make wise decisions about what to eat. *Women's Health,* Womenshealthmag.com, and my blog on mindbodygreen.com are great resources for recipes, healthy tips, and more. Once you're ready to practice mindful eating along with your yoga routines, it's wise to clear out the old to make room for the new. It's time to cleanse, and I'm not talking about your closet! A full-body cleanse is the perfect way to clean out toxins and break bad habits. Yogis often cleanse several times a year. They do this to reboot their systems (many of them do it when the seasons change, a natural time for renewal), fight off sickness, lose stubborn weight, and get back to their bodies' natural rhythms and eating patterns.

There's a plethora of cleanses out there, so how do you know which one is right for you? One of the more popular options is the Master Cleanse (often referred to as the Maple Syrup Diet). This is a liquid cleanse using purified water, maple syrup, lemon juice, and cayenne pepper. The day begins with a salt flush, continues with drinking the maple syrup concoction or water, and ends with drinking laxative tea at the end of the day. Still with me? People go on this cleanse for anywhere from 2 to 14 days, but 1 or 2 days should be enough to get you completely detoxed. I do not recommend this cleanse if you're an extremely active person, but it might be helpful if you are in dire need of rebooting your body and have the time and patience to safely let it take its course.

Juice cleansing is also hugely popular, and it's super easy to do! Just say buh-bye to solid foods and whip out the juicer or blender. Any and all fruits, veggies, and herbs can be juiced in a multitude of combinations for this cleanse. Juicing fulfills most of the body's nutrient requirements, which makes it a bit easier to keep up your energy level as you cleanse. Juicing is recommended for 3 to 10 days. It's best to ramp up before starting the cleanse by upping your consumption of raw veggies and fresh fruits, and then wean yourself off by gradually reintroducing other foods. You can also drink a laxative tea or fiber beverage (psyllium husk works well) at night to supply the fiber that's missing from your diet. This enzyme- and antioxidant-heavy cleanse helps to heal and detoxify the body safely.

Be careful of sugar content when juicing. Many beginners will go for sweet juices, believing they are healthy, and go overboard on sugar and calories.

Missing solid food already? I completely understand. I'm a huge fan of cleansing, but not of the lack of sustenance, so I partnered with Dr. Debbie Kim of Los Angeles, a holistic nutritionist, to create

The Art of Mindful Eating

a minicleanse that will reboot your system, kick bad eating habits to the curb, and help you reassess the way you look at food. Our plan is designed to not only clear your system, but also to rewire your thinking when it comes to choosing foods. A liquid cleanse works wonders, but it may leave you confused about what to eat when you return to solid food. This purification program includes both smoothies and delicious, clean foods that will leave you feeling refreshed and centered.

Start with the 3-day cleanse, and if you're still going strong, continue for 10 days. The ultimate goal is to cleanse for 21 days, because that is the amount of time needed to form a new habit

(or break an old one). We've provided recipes for 3 days and guidelines to follow if you feel inspired to carry on.

The recipes in this cleanse are an introduction to learning to cook with basic and healthy whole foods, while eliminating overly processed and sugary foods. You can use the cleanse for any number of reasons: a weight loss jump-start, healthy digestion, boosting energy, balancing blood sugars, managing blood pressure and/or cholesterol levels, balancing mental/emotional health, and skin problems. Most of all, along with your newfound yoga practice, you'll build good habits and learn how to eat healthy for life.

DR. KIM AND KATHRYN'S 3-DAY CLEANSE

There are no processed foods permitted during this cleanse. That means nothing from a box, jar, or can. The goal is to eat only fresh (and organic, if possible) foods. Feel free to be creative. Pair your salads with soups or entrées and play around—just keep it fresh! You can make two smoothies a day to serve as breakfast and/or a snack. Explore your smoothie-making power. All smoothies include a set base of ingredients (including leafy greens, flaxseed oil, and protein powder), but beyond that, it's up to you to experiment and enjoy!

DAY ONE			DAY TWO			DAY THREE		
Breakfast Smoothie (see page 36)	**Lunch** Asparagus Soup and Spinach Salad (see pages 38 and 37)	**Dinner** Greens, Eggs and No Ham (see page 39)	**Breakfast** Smoothie (see page 36)	**Lunch** Raw Tomato Basil Soup and 1 cup Arugula Salad (see pages 38 and 37)	**Dinner** Simply Delicious Salmon and Quinoa (see page 39)	**Breakfast** Smoothie (see page 36)	**Lunch** Sweet Potato Soup and Kale Salad (see pages 38 and 37)	**Dinner** Crunch Salad and Dr. Kim's Green Soup (see pages 37 and 38)
Snack So-Cool Cucumber Salad (see page 37)	**Snack** 1 cup Veggies and Dip (choose one of the dressings on page 37)	**Nightcap** 1 cup mixed berries	**Snack** Steamed Artichoke with Lemon Dip (see page 39)	**Snack** Hard- or soft-boiled egg	**Nightcap** Smoothie (see page 36)	**Snack** 1 cup Veggies and Dip (choose one of the dressings on page 37)	**Snack** Smoothie (see page 36)	**Nightcap** 1 cup mixed berries

Does This Pose Make Me Look Fat?

I arrived in Los Angeles at the ripe age of 21 wanting to pursue my dreams of acting, while teaching yoga on the side. I remember my first meeting with a manager like it was yesterday. She took one look at my 5-foot 2-inches, 108-pound frame and told me that I could be the funny best friend. If I ever wanted to play the star, I'd have to drop at least 10 pounds. Thankfully, my yoga practice came through and reminded me that life (and beauty) is about balance, not extremes.

A 2009 study published in *Complementary Therapies in Medicine* showed that practicing yoga can help women overcome binge eating. Researchers compared two groups of women with binge eating disorder and found that the group randomly assigned to a 12-week yoga program significantly reduced their bingeing behavior.

My best friend, Ashley Swider Cebulka, knows this firsthand. She struggled with a severe eating disorder from the age of 11, when she was bullied at school. For years she spiraled downward until she was hospitalized, weighing only 75 pounds. She was hospitalized two more times before she found yoga at age 20. At first, she thought yoga would be a new method of perfecting her body.

But as she continued to practice, her attitude shifted. She says, "Yoga helped me realize that there is no perfect body I need to achieve to be accepted. I am already accepted and loved exactly as I am. Most importantly—loved by myself."

Eating disorders have the highest mortality rate of any mental illness. Anorexia claims the highest mortality rate for females age 15 to 24—twelve times higher than any other cause of death. Use your yoga practice in combination with any comprehensive treatment to fight this disease and remember how to love yourself. Embrace your soul in addition to your body—you're the same person inside no matter what you weigh, so connect with who you really are and celebrate your strength and beauty!

Try these mantras when you're feeling less than confident:

- My body is perfect.

- I am the same amazing person whether I've put on 10 pounds or lost them.

- I will own my power and shape and use it to inspire confidence.

- Beauty lies in the eyes of the beholder, and I think I rock.

Recipes

Building new dietary habits is

the foundation of true and lasting health. It can be difficult to decide what to focus on—carbs, calories, fat content, cholesterol. With these simple recipes, you can learn to incorporate whole foods into your diet without sacrificing taste and satisfaction! Look for organic, free-range ingredients whenever possible.

INSTANT SMOOTHIE MAKER

SMOOTHIES ARE EASY TO MAKE AND INSTANTLY DELICIOUS! ALL SMOOTHIES SHOULD INCLUDE:

- 1–2 cups leafy greens, such as kale, Swiss chard, collard greens, beet greens, or spinach
- 1 rib celery
- 1 small Persian cucumber
- 1–2 tablespoons flaxseed oil
- 1 scoop each of protein powder and superfood powder

Blend with 1 cup of fruit and 1 cup water or coconut water to your taste.

Here are some of my favorite combinations. Feel free to experiment and come up with your own!

- Papaya and pineapple
- Strawberry and blueberry (½ grapefruit optional)
- Banana and raspberry (lime juice optional)

Salads

KALE SALAD

1 bunch kale, chopped

2 tablespoons olive oil

Sea salt

Mandarin orange slices or 1 orange, sectioned and seeds removed

½ avocado

1. Put the kale in a large bowl and massage it with the olive oil and salt. Let it stand for 10 minutes to soften the leaves.

2. Chop and add the oranges and avocado to the kale. Toss well.

3. Serve the salad with the dressing (see below) on the side.

Dressing

¼ cup apple cider vinegar

1 tablespoon raw agave nectar

1 tablespoon sesame oil

Pinch of sea salt

In a small bowl, combine the vinegar, agave, oil, and salt. Mix well.

To make it a meal, add 1 cup of cooked quinoa.

SPINACH SALAD

Spinach (1 bag)

Fennel, chopped

Hard-boiled egg, chopped

Radish, chopped

Grilled salmon

Spray a grill pan with olive oil and bring to high heat. Lightly coat both sides of the salmon with olive oil, salt, and pepper. Grill on each side for 4 to 5 minutes, or until the fish is opaque. In a medium bowl, combine the spinach, fennel, egg, and radish. Toss with Traditional Avo Dressing (see below) and serve salmon on top of greens.

Traditional Avo Dressing

½ cup olive oil

¼ cup distilled white vinegar

2 cloves garlic, minced

1 teaspoon dried thyme

1 teaspoon dried oregano

Juice of 1 lime

½ avocado

Sea salt to taste

In a blender, combine the oil, vinegar, garlic, thyme, oregano, lime juice, avocado, and salt. Blend well.

ARUGULA SALAD

Arugula (1 bag)

½ skinless, boneless chicken breast, grilled and chopped

¼ avocado, chopped

2 or 3 strawberries, chopped

In a medium bowl, combine the arugula, chicken, avocado, and strawberries. Toss, and serve with Raspberry Apple Cider Vinaigrette (see below) on the side.

Raspberry Apple Cider Vinaigrette

⅓ cup apple cider vinegar

½ cup olive oil

⅓ cup raspberries

Juice of ½ lemon

1 teaspoon agave nectar

In a blender, combine the vinegar, oil, raspberries, lemon, and agave. Mix well.

CRUNCH SALAD

Romaine lettuce, chopped

¼ apple, chopped

½ Persian cucumber, chopped

½ skinless, boneless chicken breast, grilled and chopped

In a medium bowl, combine the lettuce, apple, cucumber, and chicken. Add the Creamy-Cheesy-Sweet Avocado Dressing (see below), and toss well.

Creamy-Cheesy-Sweet Avocado Dressing

½ avocado

1 clove garlic, minced

½ cup olive oil

Juice of ½ lemon

Pinch of sea salt

1 tablespoon Bragg's Premium Nutritional Yeast Seasoning

1 teaspoon raw agave nectar

In a blender, combine the avocado, garlic, oil, lemon, salt, seasoning, and agave. Mix well.

SO-COOL CUCUMBER SALAD

3 Persian cucumbers

12 to 15 grape tomatoes

1. Trim the ends off the cucumbers and quarter them lengthwise. Finely chop the quarters. Place them in a serving bowl.

2. Use the same technique to chop the cherry tomatoes, chop and add them to the bowl.

Dressing

2 tablespoons extra-virgin olive oil

½ red jalapeño chile pepper, seeds removed, finely chopped, wear plastic gloves when handling

1 tablespoon mint leaves, finely chopped

½ shallot, finely chopped

1 tablespoon apple cider vinegar

Sea salt

Fresh cracked black pepper

1. In a jar, combine the oil, chile pepper, mint, shallot, and vinegar. Shake well to mix and pour it over the cucumbers and tomatoes.

2. Toss well and season to taste with the salt and black pepper.

Soups

RAW TOMATO BASIL SOUP

2 tomatoes, cored

3 cloves garlic

½ to 1 jalapeño chile pepper, seeds removed, wear plastic gloves when handling

1 cup fresh basil

¼ yellow onion or sweet onion

¼ cup extra-virgin olive oil

½ teaspoon salt

Ground black pepper to taste

1 cup water

Squeeze of lime juice (optional)

In a blender or food processor, combine the tomatoes, garlic, pepper, basil, onion, oil, salt, pepper, and lime juice (if using).

SWEET POTATO SOUP

1 sweet potato

2 tablespoons butter

2 ribs celery, chopped

½ onion, chopped

3 carrots, chopped

2 cloves garlic, minced

Pinch of sea salt

2½ cups organic chicken broth

1 teaspoon cinnamon

1 teaspoon cumin

1. Preheat the oven to 350°F and bake the sweet potato for 1 hour or until cooked through. Remove the skin from the potato and discard it.

2. In a skillet, melt the butter and sauté the celery, onion, carrots, and garlic for 7 to 10 minutes, until tender. Add the broth and simmer for 5 to 10 minutes.

3. Transfer the mixture to a blender or food processor and add the sweet potato pulp, cinnamon, and cumin. Blend or process until smooth.

ASPARAGUS SOUP

¼ cup olive oil

½ onion or 1 leek, chopped

Salt and ground black pepper

1 bunch asparagus, woody ends removed

3 cloves garlic, minced

2 cups chicken or vegetable broth

1 tablespoon nutritional yeast (optional)

1. Heat the oil in a skillet over medium heat. Sauté the onions until soft. Add garlic and sauté for 1 to 2 minutes. Add salt and pepper to taste. Add the asparagus and sauté until the spears turn bright green. Add the broth and simmer for 10 minutes.

2. Transfer to a blender or food processor and blend or process until smooth.

DR. KIM'S GREEN SOUP

2 cups each of Swiss chard and spinach

1 zucchini, cut into thirds

1 cup cleaned and trimmed green beans

¼ cup parsley

1. Put the greens, zucchini, beans, and enough water to cover the vegetables (3 to 4 cups) in a pot over high heat. Bring to a boil. Reduce the heat to low and simmer until the greens turn an emerald color. Stir in the parsley, remove the pot from the heat, and let it cool slightly.

2. Transfer the mixture to a blender or food processor and blend or process until smooth.

3. Feel free to add onions, garlic, or the herbs or spices of your choice.

This soup is excellent for encouraging daily bowel movements and relieving constipation.

Entrées

GREENS, EGGS, AND NO HAM

1 cup red, white, and black quinoa, mixed

1¾ cup chicken broth

2 tablespoons extra-virgin olive oil + 1 teaspoon for drizzling (optional)

2 cups water

1 cup beluga lentils

1 teaspoon cumin

1 teaspoon curry powder

1 teaspoon ground cinnamon

3 or 4 cloves garlic, minced

1 package organic baby spinach

½ teaspoon red pepper flakes

Sea salt and freshly ground black pepper

1 egg

Greens of 2 scallions or 1 small bunch of chives, finely sliced

1. Cover the quinoa with water and let it soak for 10 minutes. Drain and pat it dry. Place a medium pot over medium-high heat, add the dry quinoa, and toast, stirring as needed, for 5 minutes or until it is fragrant. Cover the quinoa with the broth, then add a pinch of salt and a small splash of olive oil. Bring it to a boil, stir, and reduce the heat. Cover and let simmer for 15 minutes or until all the moisture has been absorbed and the quinoa is fluffy.

2. In another medium pot, combine the water and lentils over high heat. Bring them to a boil and then reduce the heat to a low simmer. Add the cumin, curry, and cinnamon. Let it cook for 20 minutes or until all the moisture has been absorbed and the lentils are cooked through. In a large bowl, mix the quinoa and lentils together. Drizzle on 1 teaspoon of olive oil if you desire a moister dish.

3. In a skillet over medium-high heat, heat the remaining 2 tablespoons of olive oil. Sauté the garlic for 1 to 2 minutes, until it's golden brown, and add the spinach, red pepper, salt, and black pepper. Cook, stirring frequently to coat the leaves. Once all the leaves have wilted (they will shrink to almost one-third of their original size), remove the mixture from the pan, reserving the oil.

4. Place a nice layer of the spinach on a plate and top with the quinoa-lentil mixture. Reheat the skillet over medium heat and cook the egg sunny-side up for 5 minutes or until the white is cooked through. Transfer the egg to the top of the quinoa-lentil mixture and garnish with a festive bunch of scallion greens.

SIMPLY DELICIOUS SALMON

2 teaspoons agave nectar

1 filet wild Alaskan salmon

Sea salt to taste

1. Rub the agave nectar on both sides of the salmon and add a sprinkle of salt.

2. Cook over high heat in either a grill pan or a skillet on the stovetop or on the grill. Reduce the heat to medium-high and cook for 4 to 5 minutes on each side, until the fish is opaque throughout.

STEAMED ARTICHOKE WITH LEMON DIP

2 cloves garlic, smashed

1 bay leaf

1 artichoke, trimmed

¼ cup extra-virgin olive oil

Juice of 1 lemon

3–4 tablespoons nutritional yeast

Large pinch Maldon sea salt

1. Place the garlic and bay leaf in the water inside a steamer. Bring to a boil, add the artichoke to the steamer basket, and cook for 30 to 45 minutes, until the artichoke is tender.

2. In a small bowl, combine the olive oil, lemon juice, nutritional yeast, and salt. Dip the artichoke leaves and heart in the dressing and savor every bite!

CHAPTER 5

The Essential Yoga Poses

Every move you need for mind/body bliss

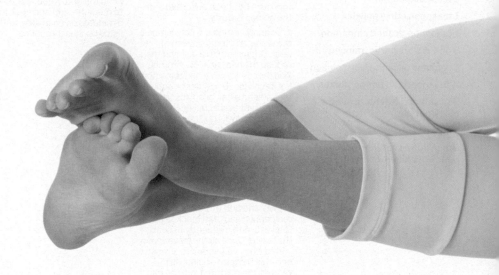

41

It's time to unroll your yoga mat

and get started! I've broken down the essential poses into various categories: Sun Salutations, Standing Poses, Seated Poses, Inversions, Arm Balances, Backbends, Core, and Restorative Poses. There are modifications shown for most poses, so you can adjust them according to your body's needs.

Remember: Rome wasn't built in a day! Take your time as you explore these poses and sequences. Engage your sense of humor and remember that the goal of yoga is to make you feel better. If you feel frustrated, take a break. Try different times of day to practice to see what works best for you. This is the beginning of the rest of your yoga journey!

The Essential Poses and Sequences

Sun Salutation A

Sun salutations are traditional

sequences of postures used at the beginning of many classes to build heat and flexibility in the body. They're a fantastic way to start your day or your workout. These moves will get you going and work out all the kinks from the day (or weeks!) before.

Join all of the following postures together to salute the sun! This routine will get your body moving in all directions to loosen, strengthen, and prepare you for a longer practice. As you flow through these poses, use the numbered steps to help you create a rhythm and remember to inhale or exhale as you move from one pose to the next. Remember, don't rush! Complete a full breath before moving on. Enjoy the process!

TIP

For all sun salutations, feel free to modify based on your needs. If you have a tender lower back, keep your knees slightly bent in standing poses. You can also place your hands on your shins or a block if the floor is too far away.

1 Mountain

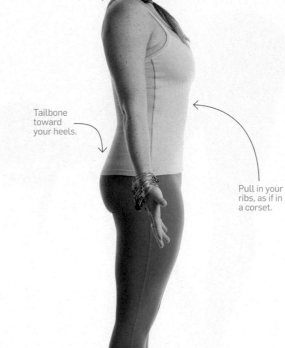

Shoulders drop down.

Tailbone toward your heels.

Pull in your ribs, as if in a corset.

- Start by standing tall, arms at your sides.

2 Mountain with Arms Overhead

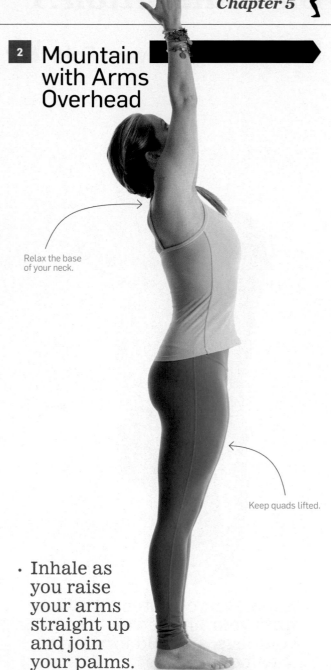

Relax the base of your neck.

Keep quads lifted.

- Inhale as you raise your arms straight up and join your palms.

Sun Salutation A

3 Standing Forward Fold ▶

4 Half Standing Forward Fold ▶

Keep hips stacked over your heels.

Elongate your core.

Keep your shoulders lifted away from your ears.

Melt your upper back and extend your heart.

- Exhale as you extend forward from your hips, straighten your legs, and fold forward to the floor.

- Inhale as you keep your hands down and extend your gaze and chest.

5 Plank

- Exhale, plant your palms flat, and step your feet back into Plank.

Reach your tailbone toward your heels.

Extend your heart and gaze forward.

Keep your core engaged.

6 Pushup

- Lower to Pushup (or jump directly into Pushup from Half Standing Forward Fold).

Draw the tips of your shoulder blades down your back.

Stay out of the base of your neck as you gaze forward.

Extend your heart.

Engage your quads.

Keep elbows in toward your ribs.

Sun Salutation A

7 Upward Facing Dog

- Inhale as you roll over your toes, and press away from the floor to lift your chest.

Press all 10 toes into the ground evenly.

Roll your shoulders back.

Lift up through your lower belly.

8 Downward Facing Dog

- Exhale, then roll your toes back over as you lift and press your hips back.
- Take 5 breaths.

Hug your upper, outer arms in.

Press your thigh bones back.

Draw your ribs in toward your spine.

9 Half Standing Forward Fold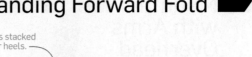

Melt your upper back and extend your heart.

- Inhale, and gaze forward as you lengthen back into your legs and bend your knees.
- Exhale, and step or jump forward to meet your hands.
- Inhale as you extend your gaze and chest.

10 Standing Forward Fold ▶

Keep hips stacked over your heels.

Elongate your core.

Keep your shoulders lifted away from your ears.

- Exhale as you fold forward over your legs.

Sun Salutation A

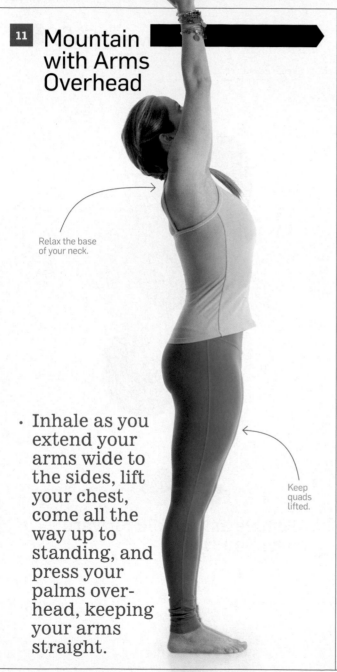

11 Mountain with Arms Overhead

Relax the base of your neck.

Keep quads lifted.

- Inhale as you extend your arms wide to the sides, lift your chest, come all the way up to standing, and press your palms overhead, keeping your arms straight.

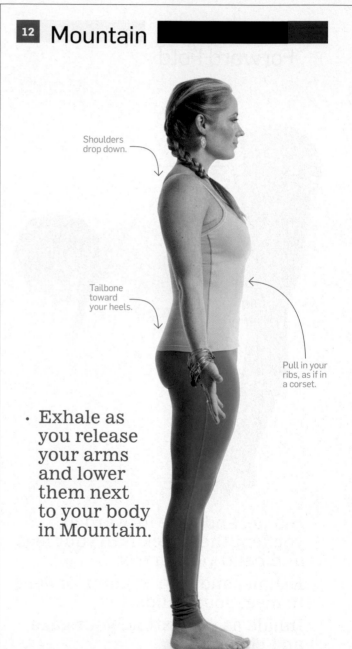

12 Mountain

Shoulders drop down.

Tailbone toward your heels.

Pull in your ribs, as if in a corset.

- Exhale as you release your arms and lower them next to your body in Mountain.

JUST BREATHE

"Don't forget to breathe." This is probably one of the most commonly heard phrases in yoga classes. There's a tendency to hold your breath in anticipation when you're overly focused on a pose. I'll hear a person take a huge gasp in and hold it, not realizing they never exhaled. The result is strain, stress, and one bright-red tomato face.

When you gain control over your breathing, you gain control over your body and your life. Our breath keeps us going every day. It smoothes out like butter when we're calm and spikes higher than a pair of Christian Louboutin heels when we're stressed. It's our body's gauge to how we react to our surroundings. Controlling your breathing brings you immediately back into a place of control. It is incredibly empowering not only because you can feel the physical and mental shift of your body—you can do it simply by connecting and focusing. Breathing is a miracle drug, my friends! Here are some simple techniques.

VICTORIOUS BREATH (*UJJAYI*)

This is the most common breathing technique used in yoga. The inhales and exhales are calm, long, and even. People often describe it as sounding like a soft wave in the back of the throat.

HOW TO: Breathe deeply in and out of your nostrils with your mouth closed.

BENEFITS:
• Lowers heart rate
• Calms the mind
• Empowers

ALTERNATE NOSTRIL BREATHING

This style of breathing is commonly used during meditation or toward the end of class as a way to cool down. The nostrils represent the two contrasting channels and sides of the body: the sun (heat) and the moon (cooling).

HOW TO: Take your right hand and tuck your third and index finger in. Place your fourth finger on your left nostril and thumb on your right. Close off your right nostril with your thumb and inhale through your left. Close your left with your fourth finger and exhale evenly though your right. Inhale through your right again. At the top of the breath, close the right and exhale through the left.

BENEFITS:
• Calms the mind
• Lowers heart rate
• Soothes headaches
• Helps to alter perspective

MEDITATION BREATH

Use this technique when you lack focus or feel overworked. It is traditionally used with a mantra: think "Sa Ta Na Ma" on the inhale, repeat "Sa Ta Na Ma" four times as you hold, then exhale on a count of 2 to release. Try it with or without the mantra and see what works best for you.

HOW TO: Take four swift inhales through the nose. Retain the breath for a count of 16. Exhale through the nose to the count of 2, and repeat.

BENEFITS:
• Clears the mind
• Builds concentration

BREATH OF FIRE

This intense breath work uses sharp exhales to cleanse and tone the belly. You'll find students practicing this in kundalini yoga or whenever they are in the need of heat and discipline. This breathing can be done seated or in any posture.

HOW TO: Start in Comfortable Seat (or Chair Pose or Plank for an extra challenge) and take a deep inhale. Quickly exhale all your air out through the nostrils by engaging your diaphragm. The diaphragm will lift in and up (as if someone punched you lightly) to push the air out forcefully. Repeat this swift exhaling (the inhale will happen without thought since you are moving fast) and continue for between 30 seconds and 2 minutes. See page 242 on how to use the Breath of Fire in my energy sequence.

BENEFITS:
• Tones the abdominals
• Aids in digestion
• Creates heat and energy
• Alleviates anger

Sun Salutation B

Sun Salutation B is the bigger, stronger

brother to Sun Salutation A. These salutes add the leg-strengthening Chair and Warrior I poses to get you even closer to the heat of the sun! This sequence is wonderful for anytime you need to break a sweat and regain focus.

TIP

Take these at whatever pace you need. If you want to slow it down, try adding a Low Lunge or Crescent pose instead of Warrior I. If you want to spice it up, try using Crow to get back to Pushup.

1 Mountain

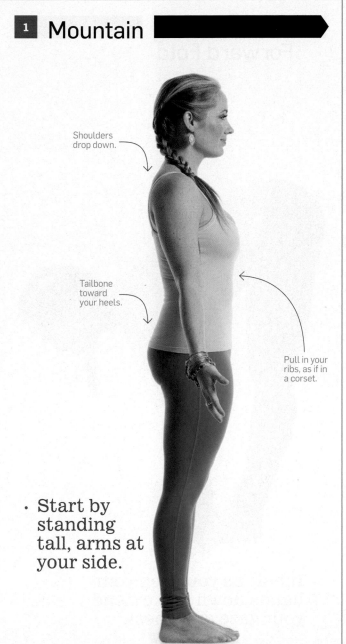

Shoulders drop down.

Tailbone toward your heels.

Pull in your ribs, as if in a corset.

- Start by standing tall, arms at your side.

2 Chair

Relax the base of your neck.

Drop your tailbone.

Pull in your ribs, as if in a corset.

Keep your weight in your heels.

- Inhale, bend your knees and sink your hips as you raise your arms straight up and shoulder-width apart.

Sun Salutation B

3 Standing Forward Fold

Keep hips stacked over your heels.

Elongate your core.

Keep your shoulders lifted away from your ears.

- Exhale as you extend forward from your hips, straighten your legs, and fold forward to the floor.

4 Half Standing Forward Fold

Melt your upper back and extend your heart.

- Inhale as you keep your hands down and extend your gaze and chest.

5 | Plank

- Exhale as you step back into Plank.

Reach your tailbone toward your heels.

Extend your heart and gaze forward.

Keep your core engaged.

6 | Pushup

- Lower to Pushup (or jump directly into Pushup) from Half Standing Forward Fold.

Draw the tips of your shoulder blades down your back.

Stay out of the base of your neck as you gaze forward.

Engage your quads.

Extend your heart.

Sun Salutation B

7 Upward Facing Dog

- Inhale as you roll over your toes and, using your arms, press away from the floor and lift your chest.

Press all 10 toes into the ground evenly.

Roll your shoulders back.

Lift up through your lower belly.

8 Downward Facing Dog

- Exhale as you roll your toes back over and lift and press your hips back.

Hug your upper, outer arms in.

Press your thigh bones back.

Draw your ribs in toward your spine.

9 Warrior I

- Still exhaling, step your right foot forward in-between your hands and spin your back heel flat so your heels form a straight line.
- Inhale as you keep your front knee bent and back leg straight. Lift your arms and torso up, gazing forward.

Relax the base of your neck.

Roll your left hip forward.

Lift out of your lower back.

Draw your right thigh bone in toward your hips.

Press into the outer edge of your back foot.

Sun Salutation B

10 Pushup

- Exhale as you lower your hands back down, step back into Plank, and lower yourself down, keeping your back and legs straight.

Draw the tips of your shoulder blades down your back.

Stay out of the base of your neck.

Extend your heart.

Engage your quads.

11 Upward Facing Dog

- Inhale as you roll over your toes and, using your arms, press away from the floor and lift your chest.

Press all 10 toes into the ground evenly.

Roll your shoulders back.

Lift up through your lower belly.

12 Downward Facing Dog

- Exhale as you roll your toes over and lift and press your hips back.
- Take 5 breaths.

Hug your upper, outer arms in.

Press your thigh bones back.

Draw your ribs in toward your spine.

Sun Salutation B

13 Warrior I

- Still exhaling, step your left foot forward in-between your hands, and spin your back heel flat so your heels form a straight line.
- Inhale as you keep your front knee bent and back leg straight. Lift your arms and torso up, gazing forward.

Relax the base of your neck.

Lift out of your lower back.

Roll your left hip forward.

Draw your right thigh bone in.

Press into the outer edge of your back foot.

14 Pushup

- Exhale as you lower your hands back down, step back into Plank, and lower yourself down, keeping your back and legs straight.

Draw the tips of your shoulder blades down your back.

Stay out of the base of your neck.

Extend your heart.

Engage your quads.

15 Upward Facing Dog

- Inhale as you roll over your toes and, using your arms, press away from the floor and lift your chest.

Press all 10 toes into the ground evenly.

Roll your shoulders back.

Lift up through your lower belly.

Sun Salutation B

Downward Facing Dog

- Exhale as you roll your toes over and lift and press your hips back.
- Take 5 breaths.

Hug your upper, outer arms in.

Press your thigh bones back.

Draw your ribs in toward your spine.

17 Half Standing Forward Fold

Melt your upper back and extend your heart.

- Exhale as you step or jump to meet your hands.
- Inhale as you extend your gaze and chest, keeping your hands on the floor.

18 Standing Forward Fold

Keep hips stacked over your heels.

Elongate your core.

Keep your shoulders lifted away from your ears.

- Exhale as you fold forward over your legs.

Sun Salutation B

Relax the base
of your neck.

Drop your
tailbone.

Corset your
front ribs in.

Keep your weight
in your heels.

- Inhale as you
  bend your
  knees, sink
  your hips, and
  raise your
  arms up over
  your head.

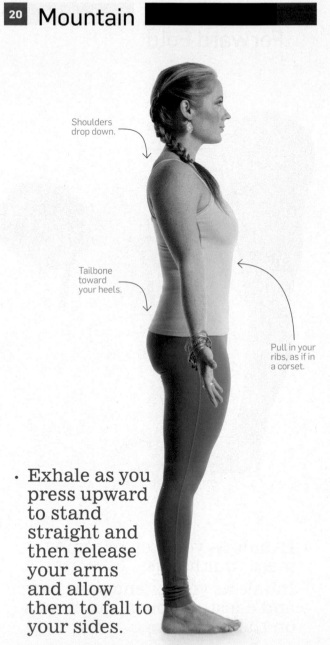

Shoulders
drop down.

Tailbone
toward
your heels.

Pull in your
ribs, as if in
a corset.

- Exhale as you
  press upward
  to stand
  straight and
  then release
  your arms
  and allow
  them to fall to
  your sides.

"Don't ask what the world needs.
Ask what makes you come alive, and go do it.
Because what the world needs is
people who have come alive."
—Howard Thurman

Standing Poses

Standing poses help us find instant
connection with the ground.

   They also sculpt and tone the entire body, leaving you with a sexy shape and confident posture. Standing poses are the bread and butter of the asana practice. These poses can be held anywhere from one breath up to several minutes depending on your needs. Classes often link several standing postures together to create a heat-inducing flow. Use these postures when you need to focus, when you've been traveling too much, or when you just want a good old-fashioned workout.

TIP
If you find yourself scattered, confused or lacking routine, hold these poses for at least a minute each. They'll help you to reconnect and feel strong and confident.

Mountain (*Tadasana*)

- Stand with your feet together and your big toes touching.
- Ground yourself evenly on all four corners of your feet.
- Relax your shoulders and lengthen your neck.
- Let your arms relax along your sides, palms to the front, and gaze forward.

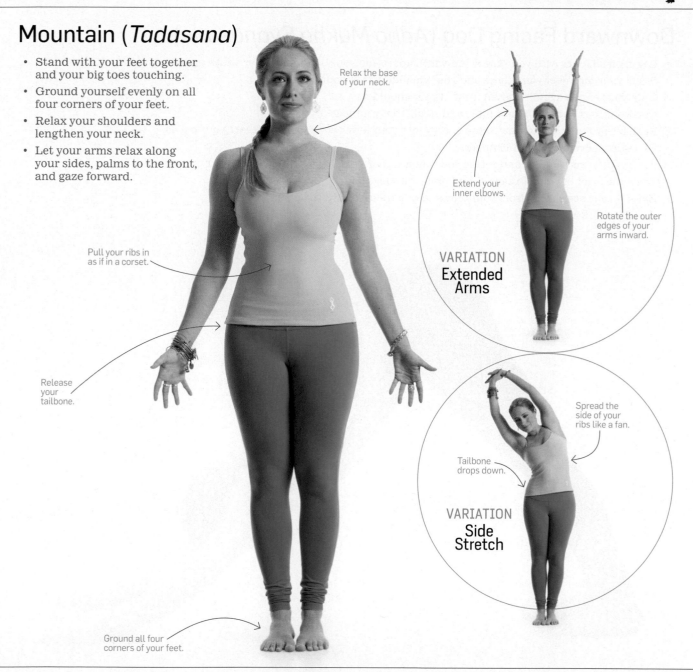

Relax the base of your neck.

Pull your ribs in as if in a corset.

Release your tailbone.

Ground all four corners of your feet.

Extend your inner elbows.

Rotate the outer edges of your arms inward.

VARIATION
Extended Arms

Spread the side of your ribs like a fan.

Tailbone drops down.

VARIATION
Side Stretch

Standing Poses

Downward Facing Dog (*Adho Mukha Svanasana*)

- Begin on all fours with your knees hip-width apart and your hands shoulder-width apart.
- Stack your hips over your knees and your shoulders over your wrists.
- Walk your hands a few inches in front of your shoulders.
- Curl your toes under, lift your hips, and straighten your legs.
- Push into your palms to draw more energy into your lower body to help elevate your pelvis.
- Press down evenly with all 10 fingers.
- Keep your arms straight and rotate your outer upper arms inward to broaden your upper back.
- Draw the front of your rib cage in and press your legs back.
- Extend your heels away from your toes and pull them toward the floor.

Cow (*Bitilasana*) and Cat (*Marjaryasana*)

- Start on all fours with your hips stacked over your knees and your shoulders stacked over your wrists.
- Keep your arms straight as you inhale, drop your belly, and roll your shoulders back (Cow).
- Exhale, press into your palms, round your upper back, and drop your tailbone down (Cat).
- Repeat this several times, performing Cow on the inhale and Cat on the exhale, to warm up your spine.

Roll your shoulders back.

Drop your tailbone.

Draw your navel gently up.

Keep your arms straight.

Standing Poses

Warrior II
(*Virabhadrasana II*)

Broaden your arms.

Keep your front knee
over your heel.

Keep your weight
in your heel.

- Start with your feet parallel and one leg-length apart.
- Rotate your left foot out 90 degrees and your right foot in slightly, so your left heel is lined up with your right foot's arch.
- Bend your front (left) knee, bringing your thigh parallel to the floor with your knee over your heel.

- Keep your torso directly over your neutral pelvis.
- Relax your lower back and keep your front ribs in.
- Keeping your inner elbows straight, reach actively with your arms to raise them parallel to the floor.
- Gaze over your front fingertips.
- Repeat on the opposite side.

Crescent (*Anjaneyansana*)

- Begin in Mountain (page 67). Step back about one leg length with your left foot as you bend your right knee to a 90-degree angle.

- Keep both feet hip-width apart, with your weight resting on the heel of your front foot and on the ball of your back foot.

- Engage your lower belly to extend your lower back and raise your arms straight up over your head, keeping them shoulder-width apart.

- Rotate your upper arms inward to broaden your upper back, and lift your gaze upward.

- If you can keep your shoulders from flaring outward and your arms straight, bring your palms together.

- Repeat on the opposite side.

Keep your hips level.

Extend through your back heel.

Keep your pelvis neutral.

Release your tailbone toward your ground.

VARIATION
Low Lunge

Tailbone lengthens back, heart extends forward, shoulders release away from your ears.

VARIATION
High Lunge

Standing Poses

Warrior III
(*Virabhadrasana III*)

Roll all 5 lifted toes toward the ground.

Extend your heart forward.

Firm your right hip in.

- Begin in Crescent (page 73). Join your palms together in front of your heart and lean forward over your front thigh.

- Keep gazing forward and lift your back leg off the floor until it is parallel with the floor.

- Extend your upper chest and gaze forward as you flex your back foot, keeping your leg straight and all of your toes pointing down.

- Stay here or extend your arms straight out in front of you and keep them shoulder width apart or join your palms together.

- Repeat on the opposite side.

VARIATION
Hands at Heart

Extend your heart forward to activate your core.

Reverse Warrior (*Viparita Virabhadrasana*)

- Begin in Warrior II (page 72) and keep your lower body in that position.
- Rotate the wrist of your forward arm to bring the palm up. Sweep your arm up and back in an arcing movement.
- Lightly touch your back leg with your rear hand, letting it land on your back thigh or calf.
- Spiral your chest open and keep your tailbone dropped to avoid pitching in the lower back.
- Repeat on the opposite side.

VARIATION
Wrapped

Drop your tailbone and lift through your lower belly.

Keep your front knee directly over your heel.

Standing Poses

Side Angle (*Parsvakonasana*)

- Begin in Warrior II (page 72). Extend your entire left side over your forward leg as you place the fingertips of your left hand on the floor to the outside of your front leg.

- Reach up with your right arm and rotate your palm forward. Extend your arm overhead to form a straight line with your back leg, rolling the outer side of your arm in toward your body to relax your upper trapezius muscles.

- Keep your chest open.

- Repeat on the opposite side.

VARIATION
Forearm

Keep both sides of your waist even.

VARIATION
Block

Place minimal weight on the block.

Relax your bottom shoulder.

Relax the base of your neck.

Draw your front hip bones up toward the base of your ribs.

Roll your torso open.

Press your front knee into your left arm.

Side Angle Revolved

- Begin in Crescent (page 73).
- Pivot your back heel flat to a 45-degree angle with the heel in and toes out. The back heel should be aligned with the heel of your front foot.
- Drop your right hand to the outside of your left foot and extend your left arm up to the sky. Extend your top palm forward and extend overhead to complete the line of your back leg.
- Keep the outer edge of your back foot rooted to the mat and your hips squared.
- Repeat on the opposite side.

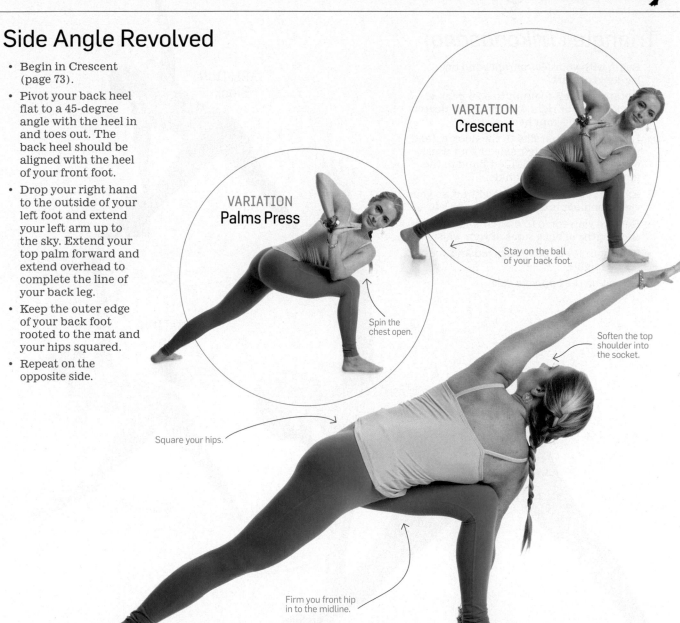

VARIATION
Crescent

Stay on the ball of your back foot.

VARIATION
Palms Press

Spin the chest open.

Soften the top shoulder into the socket.

Square your hips.

Firm you front hip in to the midline.

Standing Poses

Triangle (*Trikonasana*)

- Begin with your feet parallel and one leg-length apart.
- Rotate your left foot out to a 90-degree angle and your right foot in to a 45-degree angle, keeping your heels aligned.
- Lift your arms parallel to the floor, extend your left arm and that side of your waist forward, and move your left hand to the floor outside your left ankle.
- Extend your right arm straight up, so your right shoulder is directly over your left.
- Revolve your torso to open it and equalize the lengths of both sides of your waist.
- Keep your lower belly engaged and your legs straight.
- Repeat on the opposite side.

VARIATION
Block

Draw your bottom shoulder back.

VARIATION
Shin

Place minimal weight on your shin.

Keep the bottom of your waist extended.

Extend the bottom side of your torso over your front thigh.

Draw your tailbone back.

Keep your core engaged.

Revolved Triangle (*Parivrtta Trikonasana*)

- Start in Mountain (page 67). Step back one leg length with your left leg and turn your left foot outward 45 degrees, aligning your heels.
- Square your hips forward and place your right hand on your hip.
- Lift your left arm up into full extension and lean forward, keeping your back flat and arm reaching straight out in front of you.
- Place your left hand on the floor at the outer edge of your front foot.
- Extend your chest, then press your left hand into the floor to spiral your chest open. Extend your right arm straight toward the ceiling.
- Stack your shoulders and gaze upward.
- Repeat on the opposite side.

VARIATION
Block

Press your entire palm into a block to revolve your chest.

VARIATION
Inside Foot

Stack your shoulders.

Lean your upper chest back.

Keep your lower back level.

Press into the outer edge of your back foot.

Press your right thigh back.

Lean your upper body back.

Press down into your bottom palm.

Standing Poses

Half Moon (*Ardha Chandrasana*)

- Start in Triangle (page 78). Gaze downward and bend your front knee as you extend your front arm, bringing your fingertips to rest on the floor about 8 inches in front of your toes.
- Lift your rear leg up until it is parallel with the floor.
- Straighten your front leg and draw your left glute inward to open your hips.
- Lift your top arm straight up and stack your shoulders.
- Move your gaze upward to further challenge your balance.
- Repeat on the opposite side.

Reach tall with your top arm.

Engage your core.

Keep your standing hip firming in.

Draw your left shoulder blade in toward your chest.

Keep your shoulders stacked.

VARIATION
Block and Hip

Roll your chest open.

Sugar Cane
(*Chopasana*)

- From Half Moon (opposite page), bend your raised leg and fold it so your heel is by your bottom.

- Rotate your top arm so that your palm faces away from you as you reach back to lightly grab your foot.

- Press your foot back into your hand to open your chest.

- Gaze at one point on the floor for balance, or raise your gaze higher for a challenge.

- Repeat on the opposite side.

Powerfully press your shin and foot back.

Keep your standing leg straight.

Keep your bottom shoulder rolling back.

Curl your upper chest open.

Standing Poses

Revolved Half Moon
(*Parivrtta Ardha Chandrasana*)

- Start in Standing Forward Fold (page 49). Place your fingertips on the floor and sweep your right leg up to a 90-degree angle behind you.
- Keep your hips squared and move your right fingertips under your right shoulder so your arm is straight.
- Move your left hand to your lower back and check to make sure your hips are still squared.
- Revolve your chest to the left and firm your right shoulder blade by drawing it inward to open your chest.
- Reach up with your left arm until it points straight to the ceiling. Stack your shoulders while keeping your hips squared.
- Repeat on the opposite side.

Reach powerfully for the ceiling.

Keep your hips level and square.

Engage the entire length of your back leg.

Spiral your chest open.

VARIATION
Block and Hip

Press into the block to further revolve your chest.

Standing Split (*Urdhva Prasarita Eka Padasana*)

- Begin in Standing Forward Fold (page 49). Pop up onto your fingertips and sweep your right leg up toward the ceiling, keeping your hips squared. Inhale, and extend your chest.

- Exhale, fold over your standing leg, and brace your left forearm against your left calf.

- Engage your glutes to lift your right leg higher toward the split.

- Repeat on the opposite side.

Spread your toes.

Engage your lifted leg.

VARIATION
Blocks Parallel

Extend your chest.

Lift your left shoulder.

Extend your torso.

Standing Poses

Wide-Leg Forward Fold
(*Prasarita Padottanasana*)

- Start with your feet parallel and one leg-length apart.
- Put your hands on your hips and engage your quads.
- Keep rooting yourself in the outer edges of your feet as you hinge forward from your hips, moving your hands to the floor shoulder-width apart.
- Inhale as you extend your chest and straighten your arms.
- Exhale as you walk your hands as far back as they'll comfortably go, bending your elbows to 90 degrees and placing the crown of your head on the floor (or as close to it as you can get).
- Keep your elbows over your wrists and your shoulders lifted.

Stack your elbows over your wrists.

Draw your inner thighs up.

Keep your neck even on all four sides.

Lift your shoulders.

VARIATION
Hands at Hips

Press your hips back with your hands.

Extend your torso long.

VARIATION
Hands Interlaced behind Back

Hug your shoulder blades in.

Keep your quads lifting.

VARIATION
Hooking the Big Toes

Pull up on your toes as your toes push down on your fingers.

Draw your shoulders up and away from your ears.

Standing Poses

Standing Big Toe Extension (*Utthita Hasta Padangustasana*)

- Start in Mountain (page 67). Bend your right knee and clasp your big toe with your right thumb, index, and middle fingers.

- Place your left hand on your hip for support.

- Relax your shoulders and begin to extend your right leg straight out in front of you.

- Extend your leg as far as you can without losing your grip or straining your shoulders. Keep your hips level and lift your chest tall while gazing slightly past your lifted big toe. Keep the leg you're standing on straight.

- Repeat on the opposite side.

Soft gaze.

Relax your right shoulder into the socket.

Keep your hips level.

VARIATIONS

Open Hip

- From Standing Big Toe, rotate your right hip outward and raise your right leg to your right side, keeping your hips level.
- Gaze over your left shoulder.

Twist

- From Open Hip, switch hands, grabbing the outer side of your right foot with your left hand.
- Extend your right arm straight behind you and revolve your chest open.
- Keep your hips level and squared to the front. Relax your shoulders. Gaze forward, or look sideways for more of a balance challenge.

Fold

- From Twist, keep your right leg raised in front of you and parallel to the floor.
- Grab your foot with both hands and bend your elbows out to the sides as you extend your torso over your leg.
- Kiss your shinbone.

Hover

- From Fold, keep the lifted leg pointing forward and raise both arms straight up over your shoulders.

Drop your right hip down so it's level with your left.

Firm your left hip in.

VARIATION
Open Hip

Relax your shoulders.

Drop your tailbone.

VARIATION
Twist

Lift your heart.

Relax the base of your neck.

Extend your chest.

Keep your standing leg straight.

VARIATION
Fold

Spread your toes.

Engage your entire lifted leg.

VARIATION
Hover

Standing Pose

Chair (*Utkatasana*)

- Begin in Mountain (page 67). Bend your knees and drop your hips, bringing your weight onto your heels.
- Press your lower legs back so you can see your toes when you look down.
- Drop your tailbone, firm your front ribs inward, and lift your arms up shoulder-width apart.
- Keep your shoulders relaxed in their sockets and rotate the outer edges of your arms inward to broaden your upper back.
- Gaze upward.

Relax the base of your shoulders.

Keep your front ribs in.

Keep your weight in your heels.

Press your shin bones back.

Relax the base of your neck.

Firm your upper, outer arms in.

VARIATION Palms

Lock your thumbs, then try to pull them apart.

Straight arms.

Triceps hug in.

VARIATION Thumbs

Draw your elbows back.

VARIATION Forearms

Revolved Chair (*Parivrtta Utkatasana*)

- Begin in Chair (opposite page). Swing your left elbow or tricep to the right and lay it on your right thigh.
- Press your palms together, pointing your right elbow up toward the ceiling.
- Keep your hips even and revolve your chest open by pulling your right shoulder back.
- Repeat on the opposite side.

Press deep into your palms to revolve the chest.

Extend your heart forward.

Keep your knees even.

Lean your upper chest back.

Broaden your collarbone.

VARIATION
Arm Extended

Standing Poses

Tree (*Vrksasana*)

- Begin in Mountain (page 67). Lift your right foot, bend your knee, and grab your inner ankle with your right hand.
- Bring the sole of your right foot to your left inner upper thigh. Press your foot into your thigh and your thigh into your foot.
- Engage your core and extend your arms upward, shoulder-width apart, with your arms straight and their outer edges rotated inward to broaden your upper back.
- Gaze upward to challenge your balance.
- Repeat on the opposite side.

Keep your arms active and reaching up.

Keep your belly engaged.

Press your foot into your thigh.

Eagle (*Garudasana*)

- Begin in Mountain (page 67). Slightly bend both knees and cross your left thigh over your right thigh (like you do when you sit in a chair with your legs crossed).

- Hug your left foot to the outside of your right calf, or tuck your toes behind your calf.

- Bend both of your elbows to 90-degree angles in front of you, shift your right arm underneath your left, and join your palms together so your wrists cross.

- Repeat on the opposite side.

Press your forearms away from your face.

Relax your shoulders.

Lift your elbows in line with your shoulders.

Press your forearms toward the ground.

VARIATION
Fold

Seated Poses

Seated poses and twists do wonders

for flexibility—they release tightness in our hips and help wring the tension of the daily grind from our bodies and minds. These postures are terrific for warming up and cooling down from other sequences, too. They are most beneficial when held for at least eight breaths, and up to several minutes. Note that you should feel a sensation when attempting some of these hip-opening poses, but never knee pain—that's a sign you're going too deep. Whether you use a prop or take a lighter stance, modify each pose so you are not in any pain.

NEED A LITTLE HELP?

If you're finding it difficult to reach your feet or your hamstrings are uncomfortably tight, these simple modifications with straps, blankets, and blocks can help you adjust and get used to the poses. Don't hesitate to use support when you need it!

Comfortable Seat (*Sukasana*)

- Begin seated, and cross one lower leg in front of the other, bringing your heels under your knees and keeping your feet flexed.
- Root into your hips to lift your chest and keep your spine tall.
- Let your palms rest lightly on your knees.

Relax your face.

Soften your shoulders.

VARIATION
Blanket

Soften front ribs toward your spine.

Lengthen your spine.

Seated Poses

Staff (*Dandasana*)

- Begin seated, with your legs together and extended straight out in front of you.
- Flex your feet and root deeply into your hips to lift upward through your spine.
- Place your palms flat on the floor next to your hips, fingers forward. Hug your arms to your sides and roll your shoulders back.
- Pull your front ribs inward and your shoulder blades down.
- Gaze forward.

Keep your neck tall and even.

Lift up your chest.

Draw your front ribs in.

Press your thigh bones down.

Flex your feet.

Seated Forward Fold
(*Paschimottanasana*)

- Begin seated, with your legs together and extended straight out in front of you.
- Root into your hips and lift your chest.
- Keep your spine long and lean forward to grab the outer edges of your feet, or clasp your right wrist with your left hand.
- Inhale and extend your chest.
- Exhale and, without rounding your back, lengthen your torso over your legs.
- Relax your neck and shoulders.
- Press your thighs down and keep your feet flexed.

VARIATION
Strap over Balls of the Feet

Lift your sternum.

VARIATION
Propped Up on a Blanket

Melt the base of your neck.

Press your thighs down.

Engage your core to elongate over your thighs.

Seated Poses

Head to Knee (*Janu Sirsasana*)

- Begin seated, with your left leg straight and your right knee bent.
- Bring the sole of your right foot to rest against your left inner upper thigh. Inhale and extend your spine.
- Exhale, spin your chest over your left knee, and grab the outer edge of your left foot, or clasp your right wrist with your left hand.
- Inhale and extend your spine again.
- Exhale and fold your torso over your straight leg, bending your elbows wide and relaxing the base of your neck.
- Repeat on the opposite side.

Firm your right outer hip down.

Roll your right ribs down.

Melt the base of your neck.

Keep your gaze slightly forward.

Revolved Head to Knee (*Parivrtta Janu Sirsasana*)

- Begin in a wide-legged seated position. Bend your right knee, bringing the heel of your right foot all the way to your pelvis.
- Bring your left forearm down to the inside of your left leg and grab the inside of your left foot. Reach straight up with your right arm, spiraling your chest open.
- Rotate your right palm inward and move your top hand to your left foot, or clasp the outer edge of your foot.
- Spin your chest open and gaze up, past your right arm.
- Repeat on the opposite side.

VARIATION
Extended Arm

Soften your
bottom shoulder.

Revolve your
right ribs back.

Root your right
hip down.

Soften the
base of
your neck.

Seated Poses

Seated Twist (*Marichyasana C*)

- Begin in Staff (page 94). Keep your left leg straight and bend your right knee, aligning your foot, which should be flat on the floor, with your right sit bone.
- Inhale, sit up tall, and reach straight up with your left arm.
- Exhale, twist toward the right, and drop your left arm to the outside of your right thigh.
- Bend your left elbow so your fingertips point up.
- Roll your right shoulder back to broaden your chest, and keep lifting from your lower back.
- Repeat on the opposite side.

VARIATION
Arm Wrap

Broaden your upper chest.

TIP: *Make sure in any twisting pose that your rotation comes from your upper back, not the lower. Twisting your lower back compresses your sacrum, or the base of your spine, which causes lower back pain. Stabilize your pelvis and breathe into your chest to twist from your chest and shoulders so you keep your lower back stable and happy.*

Press your right thigh into your left arm.

VARIATION
Full Wrap

Drop your right hip down, lift your chest up.

Press into all four corners of your right foot.

Lift your chest.

Root your hips.

Press your left thigh down.

Flex your left foot.

Seated Half-Fish (*Ardha Matsyendrasana*)

- Begin seated, with both knees bent and the soles of your feet flat on the floor.
- Keeping your left knee bent, lay its outer side on the floor and bring your foot to rest next to your right hip.
- Cross your right foot over your left knee so it rests to the outside of your left upper thigh.
- Sit tall and reach up with your left arm as you inhale.
- As you exhale, drop your left arm to the outside of your right thigh.
- Bend your left elbow.
- Place your right fingertips beside your right hip or behind your tailbone.
- Press your left arm into the outside of your right knee to spiral your chest open without moving your hips at all.
- Gaze forward or past your right shoulder.
- Repeat on the opposite side.

VARIATION

- Instead of bending your left elbow, keep your arm straight and move the armpit down to touch your thigh.
- Turn your arm out and reach along the front of your shin to grab your big toe.
- Rotate your back arm inward and behind you, bend your elbow, and reach for your left hip or thigh.

VARIATION
Ashtanga Wrap

Grab your left hip with your right hand.

Clasp your outer right foot with your left hand.

Roll your right shoulder back.

Lift your heart away from your navel.

Keep your right hip heavy.

Seated Poses

Wide-Angle Seated Forward Bend (*Upavistha Konasana*)

- Begin seated, with your legs open wide in a V.
- Flex your feet so that your knees and toes point straight up.
- Keep your pelvis rooted to the floor. Inhale and lengthen your spine.
- Exhale, keep your spine long, and walk your hands along your legs without rounding your upper back.
- Grab hold of your big toes and fold forward.

Press your outer hips down.

Relax your shoulders.

Keep your quads engaged.

Extend your heart.

VARIATION
Blanket/Block

Keep your legs active.

VARIATION
Hands Forward

Roll your hips and tailbone down toward the ground.

Wide-Leg Balance (*Urdvha Upavistha Konasana*)

- Begin seated, with both knees bent and your feet flat on the floor, wider than hip-width apart.
- Grab hold of your big toes and lift both feet off the floor.
- Root into your hips to lift your spine tall, and balance on the tripod of your tailbone and sit bones.
- Begin to straighten your legs to form an upright V.
- Relax your shoulders and keep your gaze forward, or raise it upward to challenge your balance.

Extend through your big toes.

Lengthen your heart up away from your navel.

Keep your core engaged.

Seated Poses

Bound Angle (*Baddha Konasana*)

- Begin seated. Bend your knees and bring the soles of your feet together with your toes pointing forward and your heels close to your pelvis.
- Grab hold of your feet and separate the soles like you're opening a book.
- Keep holding on to your feet as you fold forward, pulling your belly toward your feet and your head toward the floor.
- Avoid rounding your spine.
- Use your elbows to pin your legs down and help your knees come closer to the floor.

Press your elbows into your thighs.

Firm your hips down.

Extend your heart.

Cow Face (*Gomukhasana*)

- Begin seated, with both knees bent and your feet flat on the floor.
- Lower your right knee, then drag your right foot under your left knee and next to your left hip.
- Lay your left leg on top of your right leg and put your left foot by your right hip so your legs mirror one another.
- Try to stack your knees.
- Reach your left arm straight up and drop your right arm down.
- Bend both elbows, swinging the right hand up your spine until you can clasp your hands behind your back. Use a strap if you cannot reach your other hand.
- Repeat on the opposite side.

Firm your upper outer left arm in.

VARIATION
Legs Wide

Keep your shins in one straight line.

Draw your left hip bone down.

Seated Poses

Hero (*Virasana*)

- Sit on your lower legs and feet with your knees touching.
- Lift your hips and move your feet to just outside your hips, then lower your bottom to the floor between your feet.
- Press all 10 toes down to the floor.
- Root your hips and sit with a tall spine.
- Rest your arms on your thighs, palms down.

VARIATION
On Block

Press your tailbone down into the block.

Relax the base of your neck.

Firm the front ribs in.

VARIATION
Reclined

Engage and lift your lower belly.

Lengthen your tailbone toward your knees.

Press your pinky toes into the ground.

Keep your knees close or touching.

Split (*Hanumanasana*)

- Start in High Lunge (page 73), with your right foot forward, and place your back knee on the ground.
- Pull your hips back to stack them over your rear knee, and wriggle your front leg forward until you can straighten it and flex your foot.
- Curl your back toes under and lift your knee, moving it back several inches.
- Wriggle your front heel forward several inches.
- Continue to switch between adjusting your front and back legs until your pelvis reaches the floor.
- Pull the hip of your front leg back and roll the hip of your rear leg forward to square your hips.
- Press all of the toes of your back foot into the floor and either keep your fingertips on the floor or stretch your arms straight up.
- Repeat on the opposite side.

Keep your lower belly engaged.

VARIATION
With Blocks

Draw your right thigh bone in toward the socket.

Flex your front foot.

Roll your rear hip forward.

Press the pinky toe of your back foot down.

Seated Poses

Single Pigeon

- Begin in Downward Facing Dog (page 68). Step your right leg forward and slide your foot toward your left, working to get your shin parallel to the front of the mat.
- Keep your back leg straight as you lower your pelvis to the floor.
- Roll the outside of your right leg down by pushing into the outside edge of your foot. Even out your hips.
- Keep your front foot flexed.
- Repeat on the opposite side.

VARIATION
Fold

Roll your left ribs down toward the ground.

Square your hips.

Roll your left hip down toward the ground.

VARIATION
Block

Press the pinky toe of your back leg down into the ground.

Double Pigeon

- Begin in Comfortable Seat (page 93). Stack your right lower leg on top of your left so your right heel rests on your thigh directly above your left knee, while your right knee is stacked on top of your flexed left foot.

- Sit up tall and hold for 8 breaths (or up to 5 minutes).

- Repeat on the opposite side.

VARIATION
Fold

Root your hips down.

Walk your hands forward, and lower your face to the floor.

Keep both feet flexed.

Seated Poses

Thread the Needle

- Lie on your back with your knees bent and your feet flat on the floor.
- Place your left ankle just above your right knee, on your quad.
- Rotate your hip open by gently pressing your left knee away from you.
- Loop your left arm through the gap between your thighs and clasp your right lower leg just below your knee.
- Move your right hand opposite your left and interlace your fingers.
- Pull your legs toward you to intensify the stretch.
- Use your left elbow to push your right thigh toward your head to get even more sensation.
- Repeat on the opposite side.

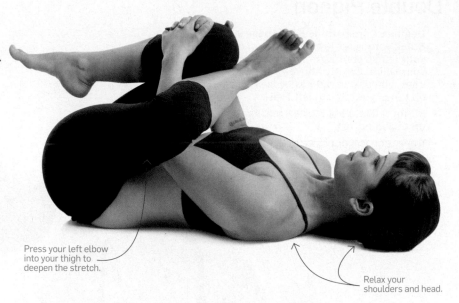

Press your left elbow into your thigh to deepen the stretch.

Relax your shoulders and head.

Happy Baby (*Ananda Balasana*)

- Lie on your back with your knees bent and your feet raised so the soles are facing toward the ceiling.
- Open your legs slightly wider than hip-width apart and grab the insides of your heels.
- Gently pull down on your heels to help bring your thighs closer to the floor beside your chest.
- Keep your hips heavy and your tailbone extended forward.
- Relax your shoulders and keep your head down.

Keep your tailbone heavy.

Relax your shoulders.

Simple Spinal Twist

- Lie on your back and hug both of your knees to your chest.
- Open your arms wide and, keeping your knees bent and together, drop them over to your right side.
- Push your left shoulder down as you elongate your lower back and turn your head slightly to the left.
- Repeat on the opposite side.

Reach your tailbone away from your chest.

Melt your left shoulder toward the ground.

Inversions

These poses may look intimidating at

first, but you can master them. The only way to be comfortable with balance is by letting go and being okay with falling down. Recognize that this isn't "messing up"—it's part of the learning process. Practice with dedication, and these poses will start to get easier. Soon you'll start to feel like a superhero!

NEED A LITTLE HELP?

If you are having trouble lifting or supporting your body when you flip upside down, practice all of these inversions against a wall for support.

Dolphin (*Makarasana*)

- Begin on all fours. Place your forearms on the mat, shoulder-width apart.
- Curl your toes under and lift your hips up.
- Straighten your legs and walk as far as you can toward your hands, keeping your shoulders directly over your elbows.
- Relax your neck and gaze just slightly forward.

> **TIP:** *This is the ultimate preparation for inversions. It builds strength and flexibility in the upper back and hip flexors. Start by holding it for 5 breaths and work up to a solid 20. Once you feel comfortable in Dolphin, then you can start working on full inversions at the wall.*

Relax your base of your neck.

Draw your front ribs in.

Press all 10 knuckles down evenly.

Firm your upper outer arms in.

Inversions

Headstand (*Sirsasana*)

- Begin on all fours. Interlace all of your fingers, tucking your bottom pinky finger in so it rests in front of your other pinky finger.
- Keep enough space between your palms so a billiard ball could fit inside them.
- Keep your fingers laced and put your hands down on the mat, keeping your wrists firm and not splayed open.
- Place the crown of your head directly behind the heels of your hands, but do not hold your head. Curl your toes under, lift your knees up, and walk your feet in toward your face.
- Bring one knee to your chest and lightly hop with the other foot to bring that leg into the same position. (You will look like you're doing a cannon-ball dive.)
- Straighten your legs up toward the ceiling, lifting with your shoulders, pressing your forearms into the floor, pulling your front ribs inward, and lifting with your tailbone.

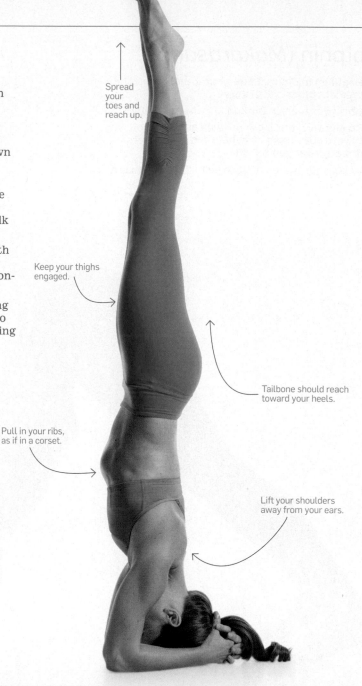

Spread your toes and reach up.

Keep your thighs engaged.

Tailbone should reach toward your heels.

Pull in your ribs, as if in a corset.

Lift your shoulders away from your ears.

VARIATION
Headstand Against Wall

Draw your heels up the wall.

Knuckles should touch the wall.

Tripod Headstand (*Sirsasana B*)

- Beginning on all fours, lower the crown of your head to the floor.
- Place your palms flat on the floor, shoulder-width apart, so your elbows form a 90-degree angle and stack over your wrists.
- Curl your toes under, lift your knees, and straighten your legs.
- Walk your feet in toward your face.
- Place your right knee on your right triceps and then place your left knee on your left tricep.
- Engage your core and lift your hips up over your shoulders as you lift your legs straight up into your headstand.
- Keep your elbows in, shoulders lifted, front ribs in, tailbone up, and legs engaged and reaching for the ceiling.

Spread your toes.

Hug your thighs together.

Pull in your ribs, as if in a corset.

Reach your tailbone toward your heels.

Pull your elbows in.

Lift your shoulders away from your ears.

Flex your feet.

VARIATION
Tripod Headstand Against Wall

Lift your tailbone toward your heels.

Inversions

Forearm Balance (*Pincha Mayurasana*)

- Begin in Dolphin (page 111).
- Walk your feet in toward your elbows as much as you can without collapsing into your shoulders.
- Keep your shoulders above your elbows and lift your dominant leg straight up in the air.
- Bend your other knee and push upward to stack your hips over your shoulders.
- Bring both legs together as you extend them straight up.
- Keep your gaze slightly forward (toward the floor) to protect your neck.

Spread your toes.

Reach your tailbone toward your heels.

Pull your ribs in.

Draw your shoulders back to stack over your elbows.

Press all 10 knuckles down.

Press into your elbows.

VARIATION
Forearm Balance Against Wall

Lift your tailbone toward your heels.

Your fingertips should touch the wall.

114

Scorpion (*Vrischika*)

- Begin in Forearm Balance (opposite page). Soften your chest muscles and shift your upper chest forward through the gateway of your arms as you simultaneously bend both of your knees.
- Keep your knees hip-width apart and the insides of your feet touching.
- Extend your gaze and lift your chin as you lower your feet by engaging your hamstrings to bend your knees further.
- Balance the extension of your chest with the bend in your knees to help you maintain your balance.

Bend your knees.

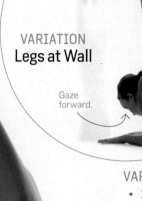

Press your toes into the wall from 5 inches to 1 foot away.

VARIATION
Legs at Wall

Gaze forward.

Broaden your collarbone.

Melt your chest.

VARIATION

- Begin in Forearm Balance (opposite page) with your feet touching a wall and your fingers facing a wall 1 foot away.
- Soften your chest muscles and lift your gaze toward the wall.
- Bend one knee and touch the wall with the tips of your toes.
- Do the same with the second leg, and align your feet so your big toes touch and your knees are hip-width apart.
- Continue to extend your chest toward the wall and gently lift as you walk your feet down it, pressing them into it to help open your chest.

Inversions

Handstand
(*Adho Mukha Vrksasana*)

- Begin in Downward Facing Dog (page 68). Shift your shoulders forward over your wrists and walk your feet several inches toward your hands.
- Lift your dominant leg up in the air and keep your gaze slightly past your fingertips.
- Keep your arms straight and firm your upper, outer arms to prevent buckling.
- Bend your other leg and begin hopping it forward to shift your hips up over your shoulders.
- Once your hips are over your shoulders, pull the second leg up to meet the other at the top.

Spread your toes.

Engage your quads.

Reach your tailbone toward your heels.

Pull your ribs in.

Firm your upper, outer arms in.

Straight arms.

Press all 10 knuckles down.

Your legs should be together.

Flex your feet as you draw them up.

VARIATION
Handstand Against Wall

Your fingertips should be 5 inches from the wall.

Handstand Scorpion

- Begin in Handstand (opposite page). Soften your chest muscles and shift your upper chest forward, through your arms, to broaden your upper chest.
- Lift your chin and your gaze.
- Bend both legs, keeping your knees hip-width apart and the insides of your feet touching.
- Lower your feet closer to your head by bending your knees further.
- Keep lifting your tailbone, and balance the extension of your chest with the bend in your knees.

Spread and reach through your toes.

Melt your chest.

Lift your chin and your gaze.

Your knees should be hip-width apart.

Press your toes into the wall.

VARIATION
Handstand Scorpion Against Wall

Your fingertips should be between 8–18 inches from the wall.

Inversions

Plow (*Halasana*)

- Begin on your back with your arms on the floor at your sides.
- Lift your legs up and swing them into the air, bringing your hips over your shoulders and the bottoms of your toes to the floor.
- Rock the outsides of your arms toward the floor to prop yourself up on your shoulders.
- Lift your chin slightly, to lengthen your neck.
- Press your legs upward to help straighten them.

Press your quads toward your hamstrings.

Lift your chin.

Press your forearms down.

Firm your shoulders in.

Shoulder Stand (*Salamba Sarvangasana*)

- Begin in Plow (opposite page). Rock your shoulders and triceps under your back so that your hips are stacked directly above them.
- Bend your elbows, keeping them shoulder-width apart, and move your palms to your lower back to help support your hips when you lift them.
- Bring both legs straight up in the air so that your heels, knees, hips, and shoulders are in one straight line.
- Walk your hands down your back, closer to the floor, to help elevate your hips.
- Keep a slight lift in your chin and gaze toward your navel.

Spread your toes.

Press into your back to lift your hips.

Lift your chin.

Firm your upper arms and elbows in.

VARIATION Supported

Fold 2 blankets into quarters and stack.

Keep shoulders on blanket but rest your head on the ground.

VARIATION with Block

Rest and extend upwards through the toes.

Stack block the tall way under the lower back.

Keep thighs together.

Rest hips completely on the block.

Arm Balances

Along with inversions, arm balances

bring magic back into our lives as well as shape and tone our shoulders and core. You don't need a gymnastic background or superhero strength to do these! You just need patience and a drive to keep going. These balance postures teach us how to cultivate focus and trust. They are the perfect blend of strength and alignment, reminding us that we posess all the tools we need to succeed—and have fun doing it!

ALICE: "This is impossible."
THE MAD HATTER: "Only if you believe it is."
—*Alice in Wonderland*

Crow (*Bakasana*)

- Squat with your knees spread wide and the insides of your feet touching.
- Put your arms between your legs and walk your hands forward until your arms are straight.
- Lower your chest to the level of your thighs.
- Hold this position as you walk your hands back toward you and hug your upper arms as high up as possible with your knees.
- Lift your hips up and lean forward so you can stack your elbows directly over your wrists.
- Keep your gaze level and pull one heel up toward your bottom.
- Keep hugging your elbows with your knees to help hold your weight as you pull your second foot up off the floor.
- Pull your heels tight toward your bottom, and round your upper back.

Round your upper back.

Press your palms deeply into the ground.

VARIATION
Straight Arms

Round your upper back.

Pull your heels toward your bottom.

Hug your forearms in.

Keep your gaze forward.

VARIATION
Block

Stack your elbows over your wrists.

Arm Balances

Side Crow (*Parsva Bakasana*)

- Begin in a squat with your knees together, balancing on the balls of your feet. Twist your torso toward your right, taking your left arm to the outside of your right thigh. Work your arm down your thigh to deepen the twist.
- Place your palms flat on the floor, shoulder-width apart, so your fingers point away from you.
- Lift your hips slightly and lean forward to bring your elbows over your wrists.
- Keep your gaze level as you bend your elbows more.
- Keeping your legs together, sweep your feet off the floor until your lower legs are parallel with the floor.
- Round your upper back and press inward with your forearms.
- Repeat on the opposite side.

Round your upper back.

Lift shins parallel to the ground.

Press into your palms.

VARIATION
Straight Arms

Stack your knees.

Keep your gaze forward.

Firm your elbows in.

Side Plank I (*Vasisthasana*)

- Begin in Plank (page 141). Bring your left palm to the center of your mat and roll onto the outer edge of your left foot. Stack your right foot on top of your left.
- Press deeply into your left palm to bring your shoulder away from your earlobe, and stack your right shoulder directly above your left.
- Engage your obliques by lifting and stacking your hips.
- Extend your right arm straight up, and gaze sideways or upward.
- Repeat on the opposite side.

Stack your shoulders.

Stack your hips.

Firm your bottom shoulder in and down your back.

Arm Balances

Side Plank II
(*Vasisthasana II*)

- Begin in Side Plank (page 123), with your right hand on the mat.
- Lift your left leg off your right and bring your knee tightly into your chest.
- Hook your left big toe with your left thumb and index or middle finger.
- Straighten your left leg toward the ceiling as you press your right foot into the floor.
- Root the inside of your right foot into the floor to help you lift your hips until the top leg is completely straight.
- Gaze upward at your left foot and keep your right arm straight, with your shoulder away from your ear and your outer upper arm firming inward for support.

VARIATION

- Starting from Side Plank II, bend your left leg and rest the sole of your foot on your inner thigh. Your left toes will point toward your right foot and your left heel toward your pelvis.
- Press your right thigh and the sole of your left foot into each other to create traction.
- Lift your hips and work the inside edge of your right foot into the floor.
- Lift your gaze up.

VARIATION
Tree (*Vrksasana*)

Press your bottom thigh up into the sole of your upper foot.

Press the inside edge of your bottom foot down.

The upper, outer portion of your support arm should be firm.

Lift your hips.

Flying Pigeon
(*Eka Pada Galavasana*)

- Start in Mountain (page 67). Lift your right foot and cross your ankle above your left knee so the lifted foot is flexed and hanging just to the outside of your left thigh.
- Bend your left leg, bringing your weight into your heel as you hinge forward from your hips and extend your torso.
- Place both palms flat on the floor in front of you, shoulder-width apart.
- Lean your right shin onto your triceps, locking your right foot around the outside of your left arm.
- Gaze forward and bend your elbows as you wriggle your left foot backward until your elbows are at 90-degree angles over your wrists.
- Lift your left foot off the floor and round your upper back.
- Extend your lifted leg behind you as if you are pushing something away. Spread your toes.

Round your back.

VARIATION
Blocks

Lean forward.

Blocks on low or medium height.

Spread your toes.

Engage your entire legth of your extended leg.

Round your upper back.

Lock your right toes around your left arm.

Arm Balances

Arm Pressure Balance
(*Bhujapidasana*)

- Begin in Standing Forward Fold (page 54), with your feet slightly wider than hip-width apart.
- Bend both of your knees slightly and drop your torso down into a fold, hugging your thighs around your arms.
- Grab hold of your right calf with your right hand. Push into your calf to help bring your shoulder behind the calf, as if you were trying to put a backpack strap over your shoulder. Repeat on the left side.
- Once you can't snuggle any deeper into your fold, place your palms flat on the floor, shoulder-width apart, fingertips facing forward.
- Sink your hips as if you are going to sit on your arms.
- Lift your heels and then your toes, and cross your ankles.
- Squeeze your arms straight and round your upper back. (This is the pressure aspect of the pose.)

Round your upper back.

Squeeze your thighs around your arms.

Hug your arms in.

Firefly (*Tittibhasana*)

- Begin in Standing Forward Fold (page 54), with your feet slightly wider than hip-width apart.
- Bend both of your knees slightly, dropping your torso into a forward fold, and wrap your legs around your arms.
- Grab hold of your right calf with your right hand and push into the calf to help bring the shoulder behind the calf, as if you were trying to put a backpack strap over your shoulders. Repeat on the left side.
- Once you can't snuggle any deeper into your fold, place your palms flat on the floor, shoulder-width apart, fingertips facing forward. Sink your hips as if you are going to sit on your arms.
- Keep your gaze forward and lift your heels first, and then your toes.
- Continue to drop your hips toward your wrists as you squeeze your inner thighs around your arms to hold on.
- Straighten your arms and your legs, reaching for the sky with your feet.
- Broaden your upper chest by rolling your shoulders back as your thighs continue to hug your arms.

Broaden your collarbone.

Spread your toes.

Lift your gaze.

Round your back.

Lift your heart.

Hug your thighs in.

VARIATION
Parallel Legs

Firm your forearms in.

Hug your thighs in around your arms.

VARIATION

- Use the same entry pose, but instead of dropping your hips toward your wrists, keep your hips elevated so your legs are parallel with the floor.
- Round your back powerfully as you straighten your legs, and hug your arms with your inner thighs.
- Spread your toes and keep your gaze forward.

Backbends

Backbends strengthen and lengthen

your entire spine and its supportive muscles and help open your hips. They're also proven endorphin-makers that allow us to open our chests and hearts. These postures help chip away at years of built-up tension in your upper back, tone your core, and improve your balance and energy.

It's important to know that you don't have to be super limber to do a backbend—you just need a good sense of alignment and patience. These poses are incredibly freeing, so go to a depth that allows space into your body and learn how to balance strength without pushing your limits.

TIPS

• Feel lower back pain when you backbend? Don't let your lower back stick out—keep your lower belly engaged and drop your tailbone down as you go into your pose. Curl your upper body and keep the base of your spine solid!

• Feel a literal pain in the neck? Don't worry about looking all the way up in your backbends. Keep your neck even on all sides and let the lifting action come from your heart. Avoid contracting in the base of your neck. Lift your chest and soften your upper back.

Cobra (*Bhujangasana*)

- Begin by lying on your belly with your legs hip-width apart.
- Place your palms flat on the floor next to your ribs, with your elbows slightly in front of your wrists.
- Press all 10 toes into the floor and engage your legs, rotating your inner thighs up to broaden your lower back, and keeping your bottom relaxed.
- Press into your palms to lift your head and chest, bringing your ribs and belly off the floor.
- Keep your arms bent as you draw back the tops of your shoulders to broaden your upper chest.
- Draw your upper chest through the gateway of your arms and lift your gaze forward or upward.

Roll your shoulders back.

Press all 10 toes down.

Engage your quads.

Lift your lower belly.

Backbends

Upward Facing Dog (*Urdhva Mukha Svanasana*)

- Begin by lying on your belly with your legs hip-width apart.
- Place your palms flat on the floor next to your ribs, with your elbows over your wrists.
- Press all 10 toes into the floor and engage your legs, rotating your inner thighs up to broaden your lower back, and keeping your bottom relaxed.
- Press into both of your palms to lift everything off the floor except for the tops of your feet and your palms.
- Drop your hips and keep your legs straight as you lift your chest straight up.
- Roll your shoulders back and draw your chest through the gateway of your arms.
- Keep your arms straight, distributing your weight equally among all of your fingers.
- Gaze forward or upward.

Lift your sternum up.

Shrug your shoulders back.

Roll your upper inner thighs up, outer thighs down.

Relax your glutes.

Press into all 10 toes.

Locust (*Salabhasana*)

- Begin by lying on your belly with your legs hip-width apart and your arms flat along your sides, palms up.
- Press all 10 toes into the floor and engage your legs, rotating your inner thighs up to broaden your lower back, and keeping your bottom relaxed.
- Engage your core and press your abs and the tops of your hands into the floor to lift your chest and legs. (The key is to lift your chest and legs to the same height.)
- Reach back with your toes as if they are trying to grab something and roll your shoulders back to help elevate your chest.

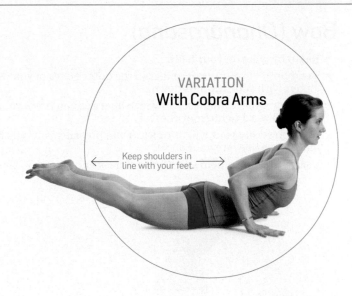

VARIATION
With Cobra Arms

Keep shoulders in line with your feet.

Spread your toes.

Extend your legs straight.

Roll your shoulders back.

Press your knuckles down into the ground.

Backbends

Bow (*Dhanurasana*)

- Begin by lying on your belly.
- Bend both of your knees and grab the outer edges of your feet or ankles with your thumbs down.
- Keep your knees and feet hip-width apart as you press your lower legs backward to lift your chest.
- Keep powering your thighs upward and pressing your abs into the mat to help elevate your chest.
- Use your arms to help you lift your knees and thighs off the floor.

Press your shin bones back.

Press your core down to lift.

Lift your quads.

Camel (*Ustrasana*)

- Begin by kneeling with your knees and feet hip-width apart and the tops of your feet flat on the floor.
- Keep your pelvis over your knees, your tailbone down, and your lower belly lifted.
- Bring your hands to your heart in the prayer position (anjali mudra), roll your shoulders back, and hug your elbows in.
- Curl your chest open by leaning back, but keep your hips over your knees.
- When you can't curl your chest back any farther, release your arms and grab your heels.
- Relax your head and open your throat.

VARIATION
Toes Curled Under

Grab your heels or try to touch them with your fingertips.

Keep your pelvis over your knees.

Relax your throat.

Lift your heart.

Relax your glutes.

Roll your upper inner thighs back.

Backbends

Bridge (*Setu Bandha Sarvangasana*)

- Begin by lying on your back with your knees bent and your feet flat on the floor, hip-width apart.
- Lift your hips off the floor and interlace your fingers beneath your lower back.
- Rock your shoulders under your chest and press into your feet to lift your hips up toward the height of your knees.
- Keep a slight lift in your chin and allow your bottom to be soft.
- Your knees should stay in line with your hips as you rotate your inner upper thighs downward to broaden your lower back.

**VARIATION
Supported Bridge**

Relax your hips.

Keep your toes in line with your heels.

Keep your knees hip-width apart.

Curl your chest.

Lift your chin.

Press your shoulders down.

Upward Facing Bow
(*Urdhva Dhanurasana*)

- Begin by lying on your back with your knees bent and your feet flat on the floor, hip-width apart.
- Place your hands, palms down, fingers toward you, just beyond your shoulders.
- Lift your hips and head up and lightly place the crown of your head on the mat.
- Hug your elbows in, as they have a tendency to splay out, and draw your shoulders into their sockets to prevent collapsing into your chest.
- Curl your upper chest backward. Straighten your arms and lift your head off the floor.
- Walk your feet in toward your hands and bring your shoulders near to or over your wrists, or as close to it as possible.
- Raise onto the balls of your feet to help you lift your pelvis.
- Draw your tailbone toward your knees to lengthen your lower back.
- Keep your hips at this height as you sink your heels back onto the mat.
- Firm your outer upper arms inward and rotate your inner upper thighs downward.

VARIATION
Blocks at Wall

Angle the blocks against a wall.

Keep your feet parallel.

Roll your upper inner thighs down.

Lengthen your tailbone towards your knees.

Press your shin bones back.

Firm your upper outer arms in.

Keep your feet parallel.

Backbends

Wild Thing (*Camatkarasana*)

- Begin in Downward Facing Dog (page 68). Lift your right leg up into the air and rotate your hip open as you bend your knee.
- Pivot toward the outside edge of your left foot as you spiral your chest and pelvis to face the ceiling.
- Drop your right foot onto the floor behind you, landing on your foot or just the ball of your foot for a deeper bend.
- Arch your chest and lift your right arm up. Extend it forward, with its inner side turning toward the floor.
- Lift your hips and let your head hang.

Release your neck.

Press into all five toes of your left foot.

Roll your top palm down to face the ground.

King Dancer (*Natarajasana*)

- Begin in Mountain (page 67). Place your left hand on your hip.
- Bend your right knee and raise it behind you. Grab the outside of your right foot at the toes with your right hand, palm up.
- Work your fingers across your toes until you are also holding the big-toe side of your foot.
- Lift your thigh and rotate your right elbow outward, upward, and then in, so it points toward the ceiling.
- Keep your standing leg straight and lift your left arm straight up. Bend your left elbow to reach back and grab your right foot.
- Once you have the foot in both hands, continue to lift your chest as you engage your right quad by pressing your lower leg away from you and elevating your thigh.
- Repeat on the opposite side.

VARIATION

- Begin in Mountain (page 67). Make a loop big enough to hold your forefoot and place it around your left foot.
- Keep your left hand on your hip for balance and use your right hand to hold the strap as close to the foot as you comfortably can, palm up.
- Rotate your elbow outward, upward, and in as you lift your thigh away from the floor.
- Lift your left arm straight up, bend your elbow, and grab the strap with your left hand.
- Press your foot against the strap and lift your thigh.
- Walk your hands down the strap as you continue to press back on it, until you eventually reach your foot.

Press your foot back.

Square your hips. Drop your left hip so it's level with your right.

Keep your chest upright.

Keep your standing leg straight.

VARIATION
With a Strap

Core

Yoga in general is full of core-
strengthening moves, but these poses cut straight to the chase. Most core work in yoga has the added benefit of toning and strengthening the shoulders and upper back, as well. (Warning: Practicing these postures on a regular basis may make you feel strong, confident, and sexy. Continue at your own fabulous risk!)

TIP
Feel pain in your lower back during core work? Keep a slight bend in your knees in poses such as Boat and feel free to prop your self onto your forearms behind your back if you're doing any leg-lowering action.

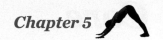

Boat (*Paripurna Navasana*)

- Start seated, with your knees bent.
- Keeping your spine long, lean back just far enough so your feet can float off the ground.
- Begin to straighten your legs together, making a V shape. Keep your arms extending forward and parallel to the ground.
- Stay balanced on the tripod of your tailbone and sit bones, chest lifted and gaze forward.

VARIATION
With Bent Knees

Keep your legs pressed together.

Keep your shins parallel to the ground.

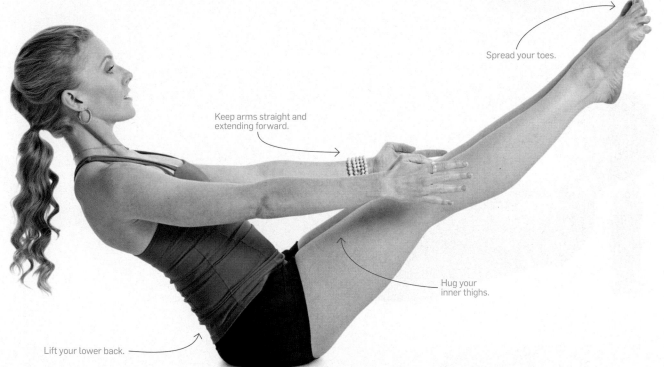

Spread your toes.

Keep arms straight and extending forward.

Hug your inner thighs.

Lift your lower back.

Half Boat (*Ardha Navasana*)

- Begin in Boat (page 139).
- Lower your body until your legs and chest hover above the ground in almost a straight line.
- Keep your shoulder blades off of the mat and hug your thighs together.
- Extend your arms and keep your gaze forward.

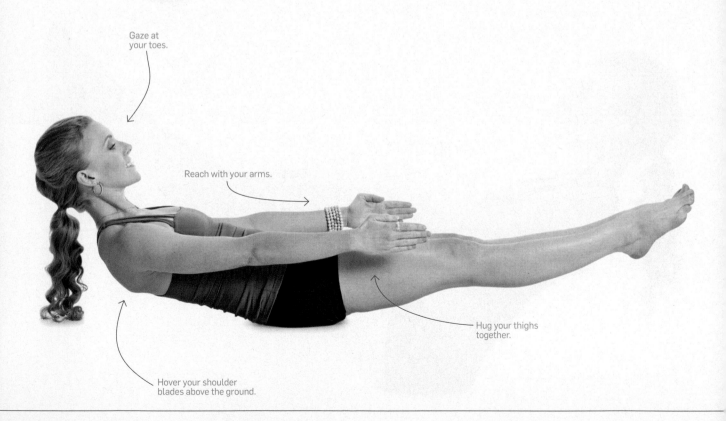

Gaze at your toes.

Reach with your arms.

Hug your thighs together.

Hover your shoulder blades above the ground.

Plank

- Begin on all fours with your arms straight and shoulders stacked over your wrists, palms flat.
- Curl your toes under and step both feet back until your legs are straight and hip-width apart.
- Bring your shoulders, hips, and heels into one straight line, with your core and quads engaged.
- Firm the upper, outer edges of your arms in to release the base of your neck and extend your chest, and distribute the weight on your knuckles evenly.
- Gaze slightly past your fingertips.

Reach your tailbone toward your heels.

Keep your core engaged.

Extend your heart and gaze forward.

Forearm Plank

- Begin on all fours with your forearms parallel to one another and shoulder-width apart on the floor.
- Curl your toes under and step both feet back until your legs are straight and hip-width apart.
- Stack your shoulders directly over your elbows. Your shoulders, hips, and heels should all be in one straight line.
- Keep your front ribs in and tailbone extending toward your heels.
- Gaze slightly past your fingertips.

Hug your shoulders in.

Gaze toward your fingertips.

Reach your tailbone toward your heels.

Reach your hip bones toward the base of your ribs.

Pushup (*Chaturanga Dandasana*)

- Begin in Plank (page 141).
- Extend your gaze forward and keep your front ribs in as you bend your elbows at 90-degree angles.
- Keep your elbows in and over your wrists, and lower your shoulders in line with your elbows.
- Keep your gaze extended and your shoulders lifted.
- Keep your upper back broad and the tips of your shoulder blades drawn down your back.

Draw the tips of your shoulder blades down your back.

Stay out of your base of your neck.

Engage your quads.

Extend your heart.

Restorative

One of the foundations of yoga is

breathing. Restorative postures help to clear the clutter in our heads and restore a sense of calm. All restorative poses can be held for a good 5 minutes (or however long it feels comfortable) in order to reap the greatest benefits with your eyes closed and your mind clear. These postures are just what you need to step away from stress, recharge, loosen up, and wind down.

TIP

The more props, the merrier! Don't be afraid to start a yoga blanket collection in these poses. Grab your bolster, blankets, blocks, straps—whatever you need to make your restorative pose the most comfortable one ever.

Legs Up the Wall (*Viparita Karani*)

- Begin seated, perpendicular to a wall.
- Bend your knees and lie back on the floor.
- Pivot your torso and extend your legs up the wall so your hips and the entire length of the backs of your legs rest against the wall. (It's optional to use a strap to tie your feet together so your legs can relax even further.)
- Let your arms rest next to you, palms up, or bend your elbows at right angles.

VARIATION
Supported Legs Up the Wall

Soften your belly.

Pull your shoulders away from your ears.

Restorative Poses

Reclined Big Toe (*Supta Padangusthasana*)

PART I:

- Begin by lying on your back.
- Keep your left leg on the floor and bend your right knee, hooking your big toe with your index and middle fingers, or use a strap over the ball of your foot.
- Straighten your right leg up toward the ceiling, keeping your foot over your hip.
- Relax your right shoulder to the floor and lengthen your right sit bone forward.
- Hold for at least 8 breaths.

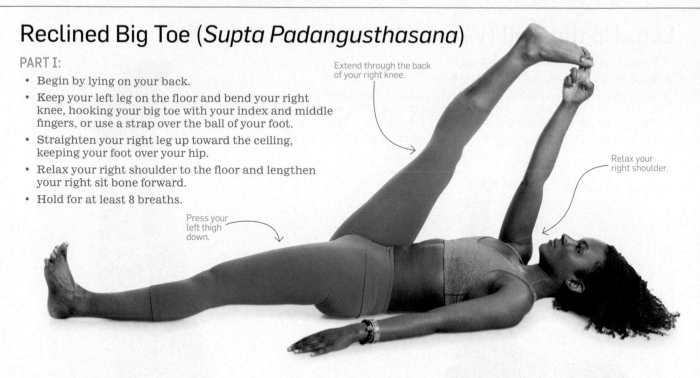

Extend through the back of your right knee.

Relax your right shoulder.

Press your left thigh down.

PART II:

- Rotate your right toes outward to open your right hip to the side.
- Place your left hand on your left hip to help root it in place.
- Keep externally revolving your right hip in its socket, and take your gaze over your left shoulder or keep it neutral.
- Hold for at least 8 breaths.

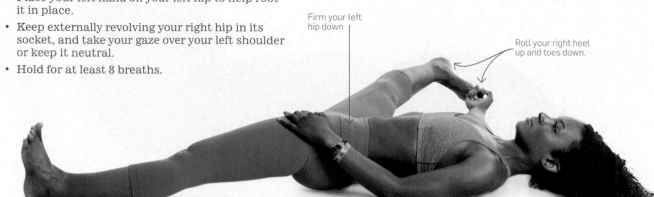

Firm your left hip down

Roll your right heel up and toes down.

PART III:

- Draw your right leg back to center.
- Grab the outer edge of your right foot with your left hand or with a strap, and lower your right arm flat on the floor in line with your shoulder.
- Bring your right leg over to the left, letting your leg hover above the floor.
- Keep the opposite shoulder rooted toward or on the floor.
- Hold for at least 8 breaths.

Press your right thigh bone away from your face.

Melt your right shoulder down toward the ground.

PART IV:

- Lift your right leg back to center and grab hold of your calf or foot with both hands.
- Keep both shoulders relaxed as you gently bring your leg toward you.
- Keep your head on the floor and your right leg as straight as possible.
- Hold for at least 8 breaths.
- Repeat all four parts on the opposite side.

Flex your left foot.

Soften your shoulders.

Restorative Poses

Reclined Bound Angle (*Supta Baddha Konasana*)

- Begin on your back, with your knees bent wide and the soles of your feet together.
- Bring your heels as close to your pelvis as you comfortably can.
- Lift your chest and draw your shoulder blades down your back to lengthen your neck.
- Take your arms wide, with your palms facing up.

VARIATION
**With a Bolster,
Two Blankets, and a Strap**

Melt your inner thighs.

Child's Pose (*Balasana*)

- Sit on your lower legs with your knees and feet touching.
- Fold your torso over your thighs and rest your forehead on the floor.
- Lay your arms along your sides with your palms facing up.
- Completely relax your shoulders and neck.

TIP: *If this feels too tight, separate your knees hip-width apart but keep your feet touching. This will give you more space in your chest. You can also place a blanket between your heels and bottom to alleviate tightness in your hips.*

Melt your chest.

Roll your shoulders down.

Corpse (*Savasana*)

- Lie on your back.
- Let your legs and arms flop open with your palms facing up.
- Lift your chest to snuggle your shoulder blades down your back. Release all tension in your body.
- Close your eyes (or, even better, cover them with a cloth) and bring your breathing back to normal.
- Empty your mind. Take a rest.

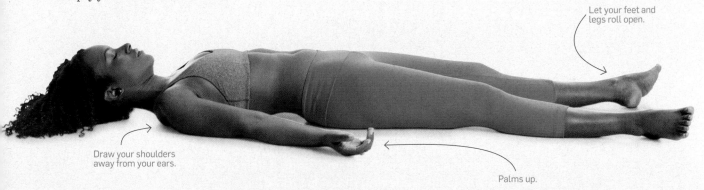

Let your feet and legs roll open.

Draw your shoulders away from your ears.

Palms up.

More Essential Poses

In addition to the traditional yoga

poses in this chapter, I've added a few more that I incorporate into the sequences in this book. Some (like Windshield Wiper Abs) are designed as mini-exercises, and some (like Finger Stretches) target specific areas of concern. Feel free to use any of these in your daily routine as part of a sequence or on their own. The great thing about yoga is the ability to modify poses or incorporate other stretches and movements into your routine—making it incredibly easy to switch it up and have fun with it!

TIP

Remember, there is a variation to every pose that will suit your needs. Listen to what your body needs and drop your ego. It reminds me of this Albert Einstein quote: "Everyone is a genius. But if you judge a fish on its ability to climb a tree, it will live its whole life believing that it is stupid."

Lower-Belly Lifts

- Lie flat on your back with both legs straight up in the air.
- Lie your arms flat next to your sides with the palms down and shoulders relaxed.
- Exhale as you lift your hips a few inches off the ground.
- Inhale as you lower back down.

Spread your toes.

Hug your thighs together.

Relax your face.

Keep your shoulders rooting down.

More Essential Poses

Windshield-Wiper Abs

- Lie flat on your back with both legs straight up in the air.
- Rest your arm straight and wide on the ground so that the palms are facing down and in line with your shoulders.
- Exhale, and keep your legs straight and together as you reach your toes toward the opposite fingers.
- Inhale to come back up to center, and then switch sides.

Extend your tailbone.

Root your opposite palm down.

Keep your shoulders heavy.

Fingertips Abs

- Lie flat on your back with both legs straight up in the air.
- Keep your right leg up and lower your left leg, keeping it straight until it hovers above the ground.
- As you exhale, curl your head and chest off the ground and extend you arms forward.
- Hold this position or, if possible, join your fingertips together in front of your right hamstring.

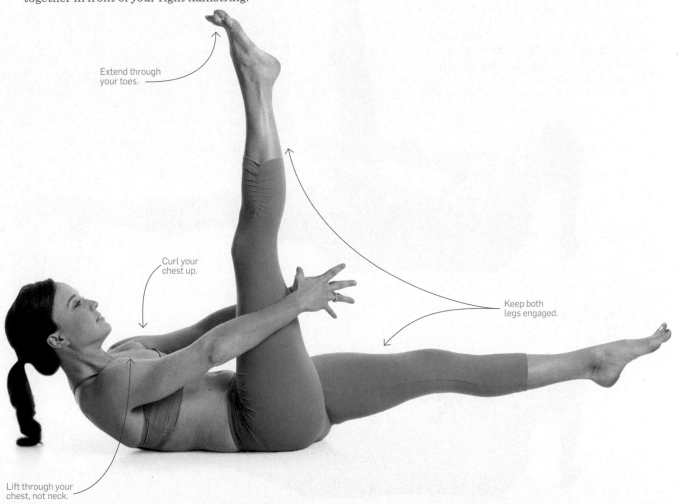

Extend through your toes.

Curl your chest up.

Keep both legs engaged.

Lift through your chest, not neck.

More Essential Poses

Twisted Lowering Abs

- Lie flat on your back with both legs straight up in the air.
- Keep your right leg up and lower your left leg, keeping it straight until it hovers above the ground.
- As you exhale, curl your head and chest off the ground and extend your arms to the outside of your right thigh, interlacing your fingers.
- Exhale as you hold your twist and lower your top leg to meet your bottom leg.
- Inhale as you lift your right leg back up to its original position.

Keep your legs straight and active.

Keep your right shoulderblade lifted.

Tiny Little Package

- Lie on your back and draw both knees into your chest.
- Grab your shins, pulling your legs tight to your chest and drawing your forehead or even nose toward your knees so that your head leaves the ground.
- Relax your shoulders.

Hug your legs in tight.

Lift up your shoulderblades.

More Essential Poses

Gentle Seated Twist

- Begin in Comfortable Seat (page 93). Place your right fingertips behind your tailbone to help prop yourself up tall.
- Reach your left wrist to the outside of your right thigh.
- Press your left wrist gently into your leg to revolve your chest open.

Roll your right shoulder back.

Twist in your upper chest, not in your lower back.

Keep your spine tall.

Stay even and rooted in your hips.

Puppy Dog

- Start on all fours with your knees hip-width apart and hands shoulder-width apart.
- Stack your hips above your knees and walk your arms out in front of you, keeping your arms straight.
- Melt your belly, chest, and throat down toward the ground.
- Hug the upper outer arms in and press into your palms.
- Gaze forward.

Keep your hips over your knees.

Melt your chest toward the ground.

Bend your elbows until you can rest your forehead on the ground.

Goddess

- Start with your feet one leg's distance apart and your feet parallel.
- Rotate your heels in and toes out until your knees point in the same direction as your toes.
- Bend your knees, and drop your pelvis into a neutral position.
- Keep your arms lifted, elbows slightly bent, and palms up.
- You can add a mudra (page 294) or keep your palms open.

Relax your shoulders.

Keep your knees in line with your toes.

Drop your tailbone and keep your lower belly lifted.

More Essential Poses

Knee-to-Nose

- Begin in Downward Facing Dog (page 68). Lift your right leg up into the air.
- Bring your shoulders over your wrists, keeping your arms straight, and draw your right knee tight into your chest.
- Try to kiss your knee as you press the ground away and round your back.

Keep your hips in line with your shoulders.

Press the ground away.

Draw your heel toward your bottom.

Faith HUNTER

Faith Hunter incorporates her Louisiana upbringing, modern mystical sounds, and the purity of breath into her yoga philosophy. She began practicing yoga back in the early '90s, during the time her older brother, Michael, was losing his battle with HIV/AIDS. Yoga gave Faith the tools and confidence she needed to deal with the grief and negativity surrounding her brother's death. It provided her with the internal strength to move forward in difficult times, and helped quiet her mind and keep focused on the positive aspects of life. She views everything as an opportunity to learn something new.

Yoga can be transformative, but for Faith, that didn't mean becoming a different person—it meant reminding her of who she is at her core. It helped her return to a sense of openness, adventure, and passion. It allowed her to view her body as an extension of her heart and motivate her to live life to the fullest.

"Moments of playfulness and adventure are fully reflected in my yoga practice and teaching. I make every attempt to enjoy life as it comes. My practice reconnects my spirit, mind, body, and mood."

Faith has appeared on the cover of Yoga Journal *and has contributed to* OmYoga & Lifestyle *magazine in the UK. Faith is a social advocate, writer, and yoga podcaster, and she leads yoga teacher trainings throughout the year. She is the owner of Embrace, a yoga studio located in Washington, D.C. You can practice with Faith around the globe, or find her online at faithhunter.com.*

More Essential Poses

Half Dog at Wall

- Stand facing a wall with your feet hip width apart.
- Place your palms shoulder-width apart on the wall and walk your hands down until your torso is parallel with the ground.
- Draw your front ribs in, lift your lower belly and lengthen your lower back to take any arch out.
- Press evenly into all of your knuckles as you firm the upper outer edges of your arms in and around the bone (show 'action arrows' on the picture).
- Keep the outer side of your shoulders and sides long while the inner shoulders and base of the neck relax.

Roll your outer arms down and in.

Press evenly into all 10 knuckles.

Keep your ribs pulled in.

Finger Stretches

- Flip your right palm up and flex your wrist so that your fingers point down.
- Using your left hand, gently pull one finger back at a time so the nail side is folding back toward the front of the wrist.
- Pull with just enough traction to create some sensation.
- Repeat on your other hand.

VARIATION

- From standing, bend your elbows and press your knuckles into each other behind your back.
- Roll your hands in an upward motion until the palms flip together with the fingers pointing upward.
- Swim your hands up your spine as much as you comfortably can.
- Press the knuckles together and roll your shoulders back.

VARIATION
Anjali Mudra Regular Behind the Back

CHAPTER 6
Total Body Yoga
A series of targeted workouts you can do in 15 minutes or less

In a perfect world, we'd have

a full 90 minutes a day to explore our yoga practice, followed by a luxurious organic meal and the rest of the day free to meditate and relax. Oh, and George Clooney would be there. Well, that's called a yoga retreat—"retreat" being the key word. The reality is that we are all busy people with jobs to do, places to go, and often a crazy, jam-packed schedule. Not to mention the fact that yoga studios and retreats can cost a pretty penny!

To give you the benefit of a full session when you don't have much time, I've designed several sequences that take 15 minutes or less. They target specific areas of the body, so you can focus on what needs the most work or where you feel you're holding stress. Once you have a good grip on the sequences, you can customize how long you hold the postures and even add your own spin by including other postures or transitions.

Get to know these routines and you'll never have to sacrifice yoga on a busy day again! No matter how much or how little time you can devote to your practice each day, you should feel accomplished every time you decide to unroll your mat. George would be proud.

15-Minute Sequences

A.M. *Yoga*

Coffee schmoffee. Kick that caffeine

addiction to the curb with this energy-inducing sequence that will start your day off right. It incorporates feel-good stretches followed by strong standing poses that literally make sure you get out of bed on the right foot. A final Handstand reminds you to take on the challenges of the day with a playful, open spirit.

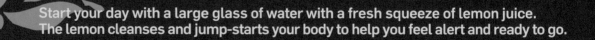

TIP
Start your day with a large glass of water with a fresh squeeze of lemon juice. The lemon cleanses and jump-starts your body to help you feel alert and ready to go.

1

Child's Pose
(page 149)

2

Keep your
hips over
your knees.

Melt your chest
and throat toward
the ground.

Press
down
into all
10 toes.

Keep your
arms straight.

Puppy Dog Stretch
Start with Puppy Dog (page 156), then make these adjustments.

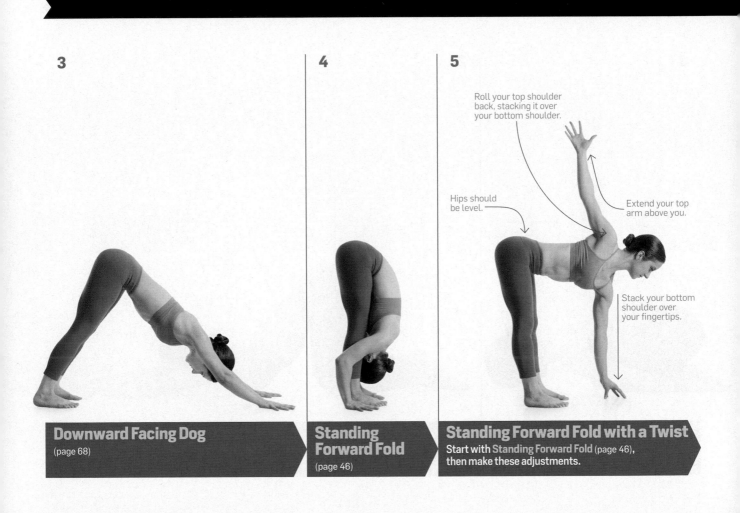

3

Downward Facing Dog
(page 68)

4

Standing Forward Fold
(page 46)

5

Roll your top shoulder back, stacking it over your bottom shoulder.

Hips should be level.

Extend your top arm above you.

Stack your bottom shoulder over your fingertips.

Standing Forward Fold with a Twist
Start with **Standing Forward Fold** (page 46), then make these adjustments.

6

Warrior II
(page 72)

7

Reverse Warrior
(page 75)

8

Triangle
(page 78)

9

Half Moon
(page 80)

10

11

12

Standing Split
(page 83)

Handstand
(page 116)

Vinyasa
(page 183)

Repeat the entire sequence starting with Step 6.

P.M. *Yoga*

Can I tempt you with a yoga nightcap?

After you've performed these poses, slip into your pj's and prepare yourself for blissful sleep. This sequence releases lower-back tension, opens your hips after long hours on your feet, and melts your upper back to lift the weight of the day off your shoulders. Focus on relaxing your breathing and letting go of the day's agenda. If you're looking for deeper relaxation, try holding steps 5, 6, and 7 for 5–10 minutes each.

TIP

Hold the last two poses for at least 5 minutes each. Try placing an eye pillow over your eyes or a cool towel over your face to help you relax and find calm. For pure bliss, soak a towel in water and sprinkle a few drops of lavender oil before placing it on your face.

1

2

Place a block at medium height and wide under your shoulderblades.

Let both shoulders melt into the ground.

Place a block at a high height under your head.

Shoulder Opener
Start with Reclined Bound Angle (page 102), then make these adjustments.

Reclined Twist with Legs Together
Start with Simple Spinal Twist (page 109), then make this adjustment.

3

4

Keep your spine long.

Reclined Big Toe
(page 146)

Eagle Arms
Start seated cross legged with Eagle (page 91),
then make these adjustments.

5

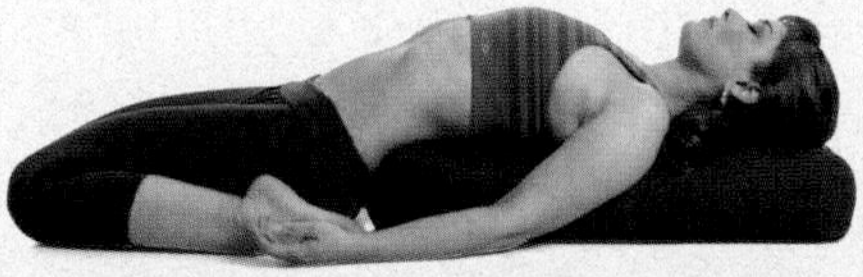

6

7

Reclined Hero
(page 104)

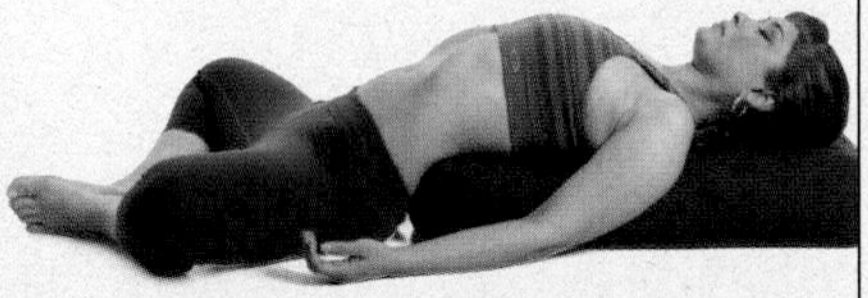

Reclined Bound Angle
(page 102)

Legs Up the Wall
(page 145)

Arms Sequence

Yoga helps to calm the mind and

spirit, but it also creates absolutely gorgeous arms! Many of the postures here help build your strength in the upper back and shoulders without adding bulk. The result is long, lean muscles that match your body type and will give you so much confidence you'll only ever want to wear sleeveless dresses.

TIP

Every day is different. Don't tackle your yoga practice with the same vigor every day, make sure you adjust the poses and modify them to fit your mood, both physically and mentally. If you feel strong—go for it! Add extra holds and challenging variations. But if you're tired or feeling weak, don't be afraid to modify them. You can always practice Plank and Pushup with your knees on the floor for additional support. Know when holding back is the strong choice.

1

Half Dog at Wall
(page 160)

2

Downward Facing Dog
(page 68)

Arms Sequence

3

Plank
(page 141)

4

Cross your ankles.

Drop your knees to the ground.

Engage your lower belly.

Pushup on Knees
Start with Pushup (page 143), then make these adjustments.

5

6

Elbows bend wide.

Fingertips spin in toward
a 45-degree angle.

Revolved Pushup
Start with **Pushup** (page 143),
then make these adjustments.

Pushup
(page 143)

Arms Sequence

7

Forearm Plank
(page 142)

8

Spread your toes.

Lift one leg high, then repeat on the other side.

9

Dolphin with One-Leg Lift
Start with Dolphin (page 111), then make these adjustments.

Side Plank
(page 123)

Arms Sequence

10

Vinyasa
(page 183)

VINYASA FLOW

"Vinyasa" translates as "the connection of breath to movement." In vinyasa flow yoga, the vinyasa is a series of postures linked together to help build and maintain heat. In the sequences in this chapter, the vinyasa is the linking of Plank into Pushup, lifting into either Cobra or Upward Facing Dog and then pulling the hips back into Downward Facing Dog. This is a mini-sequence that can be repeated anywhere from once or twice to 30 times per session. Vinyasa will get you strong and flexible fast, but make sure you're not rushing through it or collapsing your shoulders and lower back. Pay attention to your alignment, and always connect your breath to the movement. If you lose your breath and decide to keep going, it might still be a workout—but it's no longer yoga.

Tips for a Perfect Vinyasa

- Keep your gaze forward in Plank and Pushup. This will help you extend your chest and keep your back flat. You want to avoid any rounding in your upper back, which stresses out your trapezius muscles.
- Keep your elbows tight against your ribs in Pushup, and engage your lower belly before you lower. This will help if you have lower-back pain or a hyperflexible lower spine.
- Don't let your shoulders dip below the height of your elbows in Pushup. Keep resisting the lowering with your shoulders so you don't wear out your shoulder joints.
- Look up with your eyes, instead of with your entire head, in Cobra and Upward Facing Dog. This will help you relax the base of your neck. Remember, lifting your chest doesn't also mean lifting your shoulders! Avoid the "turtleneck" syndrome: Keep your shoulders down and away from your earlobes, and let your sternum do the lifting. This will feel much better.

11

Child's Pose
(page 149)

Legs Sequences

All standing poses can bring on a major

burn, depending on how long you choose to hold them. Both of these sequences work your quads and glutes, creating strong, lean legs. You can do them separately or combine for an extra workout. To maximize your leg work in a limited time, I've linked together the Warrior I, Warrior II, Reverse Warrior, and Side Angle poses. Try doing them for 5 breaths at a time at first. Eventually increase the hold to 8 breaths, and then to 2 minutes.

If you're looking to add more movement, hold each pose for 1 breath, linking them in this order: Warrior I, Warrior II, Reverse Warrior, Side Angle. At the end of these four poses, add a vinyasa sequence and repeat on the opposite side. This is called a Dancing Warrior sequence.

CHILD'S POSE TIP

Feel free to take a break in Child's Pose throughout your practice, whenever you lose your breath or feel overworked. Take 5–8 breaths in this pose, then move back into your sequence.

Crescent Sequence

1

Downward Facing Dog
(page 68)

2

Relax the base of your neck.

Keep arms alongside your ears.

Keep your core engaged.

Your belly should hover above your thigh.

Crescent with Arms Forward
Start with **Crescent** (page 73), then make these adjustments. Hold for 5 breaths.

Crescent Sequence, continued

3

Keep arms alongside your hips with palms facing in.

Extend through heel.

Keep your weight in your heel.

Crescent with Arms Back
Start with Crescent (page 73), then make these adjustments.
Hold for 5 breaths.

4

Crescent
(page 73)
Hold for 5 breaths.

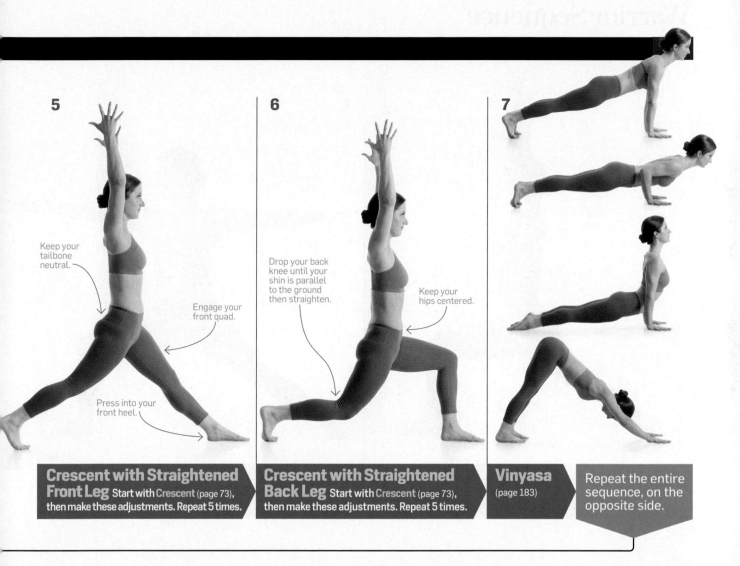

5

Keep your tailbone neutral.

Engage your front quad.

Press into your front heel.

Crescent with Straightened Front Leg Start with Crescent (page 73), then make these adjustments. Repeat 5 times.

6

Drop your back knee until your shin is parallel to the ground then straighten.

Keep your hips centered.

Crescent with Straightened Back Leg Start with Crescent (page 73), then make these adjustments. Repeat 5 times.

7

Vinyasa (page 183)

Repeat the entire sequence, on the opposite side.

Legs Sequences

Warrior Sequence

1

Warrior I
(page 71)

2

Warrior II
(page 72)

3

Reverse Warrior
(page 75)

4

Side Angle
(page 76)

Warrior Sequence, continued

5

Warrior II
(page 72)

6

Vinyasa
(page 183)

Repeat the sequence starting with step 1 on opposite side, then continue to step 7.

Legs Sequences

Warrior Sequence, continued

7

Crescent into Warrior III
(page 73–74)

Repeat on each side and hold for 5 breaths.

8

Standing Forward Fold
(page 46)

9

Legs Up the Wall
(page 145)

Core Sequence

Let's face it—we all want the benefits

of a strong core and bikini-worthy abs, without all the pain of the workouts that create them! Unfortunately, there's no way around it: Strong core work requires effort, so pack your sense of humor for this one. Pretend you're a ninja as you move through this sequence and you'll get through it in no time—strong, calm, quiet, and slick! Remember that sexy abs are strong and confident, so own your hard-won shape—that's hot.

TIP

Don't rush! The goal here isn't to see how many reps you can pump out in a short amount of time. This often leads to bad posture, poor alignment, and often, injury. Take the time to breathe and make your movements thoughtful and precise. You'll burn more energy and target exactly where you want to tone up and tighten.

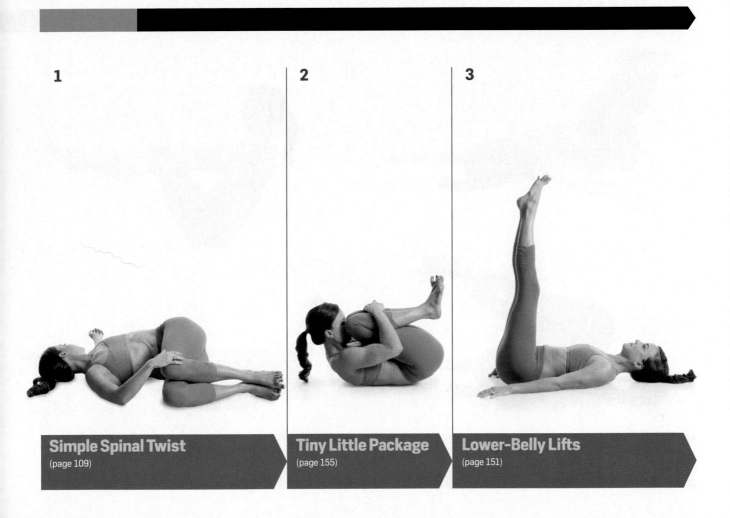

1

Simple Spinal Twist
(page 109)

2

Tiny Little Package
(page 155)

3

Lower-Belly Lifts
(page 151)

Core Sequence

4

Windshield-Wiper Abs
(page 152)

5

Boat with Bent Knees into Half Boat
(page 139)
Hold for 5 breaths. Repeat 5 times.

JUMPING THROUGH TO SIT

Vinyasa can be used to link standing or seated postures. When you perform vinyasa in seated postures, you'll want to jump through to a seated position instead of stepping forward into a posture. Learning this transition takes practice, flexibility, and patience. Depending on your body type you may get it on the first try or have a lifelong project ahead of you. The good news is, there are some tricks! Grab two blocks and unroll your mat.

Have you ever seen a duck land in water? Right before they come in for the landing they stick their little webbed heels out in front of them so they land heels first. This technique creates a splashless and graceful landing. Jumping through to sit is similar, so channel your best impersonation of a duck and give it a go!

Come into Downward Facing Dog with your hands on blocks set up at the low height shoulder-width apart so you can land your hips between them. Step your feet together and look way past your hands to where your feet will eventually land. Keep your eyes on this one spot and lift your tail high into the air as you come onto the balls of your feet. Bend your knees and do a light hop up, pulling your thighs as close to your torso as you can, and flex your feet as they pass through the blocks. Keep pressing your hands into the blocks to pull more strength into your core. Let your heels land first, then your bottom.

Some people find jumping with straight legs difficult. The "flexing" element of the jump might make you land on your feet instead of continuing through to a sitting position. Keep trying. It really does take practice and time. If you know your hamstrings are tight and not ready to be straight, let your knees bend and your ankles cross as you do your jump.

6

Vinyasa and Jump Through to Lie Down
(page 183 and on this page)

Core Sequence

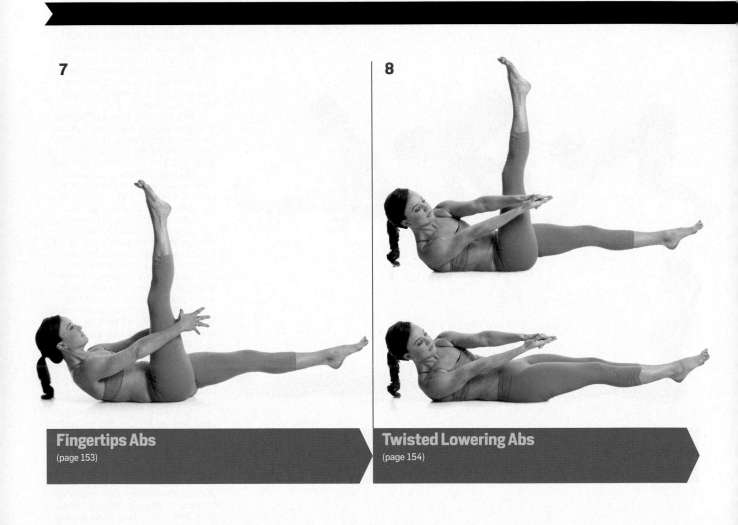

7

Fingertips Abs
(page 153)

8

Twisted Lowering Abs
(page 154)

9

Vinyasa and Jump Through to Sit
(page 183 and 197)

Core Sequence

10

11

Bridge
(page 134)

Corpse (Savasana)
(page 149)

TIFFANY
Cruikshank

An internationally celebrated yoga teacher, author, and health and wellness expert, Tiffany Cruikshank travels the globe inspiring people to live their lives to the fullest. She is known for her lighthearted attention to detail and passionate dedication to the practice.

Tiffany started practicing yoga when she was 14 years old and was instantly enthralled by the physical challenge. She quickly noticed her yoga practice gave her a comfort in her own skin. As a woman, yoga has helped her establish a healthy body image and appreciate the "perfect imperfections" that make her who she is.

> **"Yoga gives me a sense of courage and confidence when life flips things upside down, a sense of stability when life shakes things up and a sense of clarity in an overwhelming world. I am forever grateful for this practice and the many ways it has transformed my life and my perspective."**

Tiffany is the acupuncturist and yoga teacher at the Nike World Head-quarters in Portland, Oregon. She has been featured in video and print ads for Nike, Lululemon, Yogi Tea, and KiraGrace. Her classes can be found on YogaGlo.com. She has written many articles on MindBodyGreen.com, Origin Magazine, and ElephantJournal.com, and is the author of Optimal Health for a Vibrant Life, a 30-day detox for yogis. www.TiffanyYoga.com.

Butt

There are some seriously cute and

stylish yoga pants out there that can take you from mat to cocktails, but here's the catch—they're all pretty tight. This is ultimately a good thing because you don't want to trip on fabric as you move from twist to fold to inversion. The somewhat unsettling part is that your backside is totally on display! Fear not, my courageous friend. Yoga and stretchy pants were made for one another. Tackle this sequence and your buns will be stealing the show—in yoga pants or skinny jeans.

1

Standing Forward Fold
(page 46)

2

Stack your hip
over your leg.

Hook your toe and lift your leg
so it's parallel to the ground.

Side Leg Lift
Start with Standing Forward Fold (page 46),
then make these adjustments.

Carpal Tunnel Syndrome

Carpal tunnel syndrome is a condition

that causes tingling, numbness, and pain in the hands and wrists. It's often the result of spending too much time at a computer keyboard (hello, those of you who are obsessed with Facebook!). The bad news is that because so many of us use computers now, in addition to using our hands for everything else, it's a tricky injury to avoid. The good news is that yoga can come to the rescue! A 1988 study in the *Journal of the American Medical Association* showed that people who practiced 11 yoga postures twice weekly for 2 months had better grip strength and greater lessening of pain than a control group that did no yoga. But don't pop into a celebratory Handstand quite yet!

The idea of subjecting your wrists to poses like Plank and Downward Facing Dog can make handcuffs sound alluring, so try these variations and postures to help you get back on track. You'll be cartwheeling pain-free in no time.

TIP

If your wrists bother you, try using an ace bandage to support and keep your wrists stable, or practice with a wedge block to alleviate the pressure. You can always drop onto your forearms or knees in poses such as Plank and Downward Facing Dog.

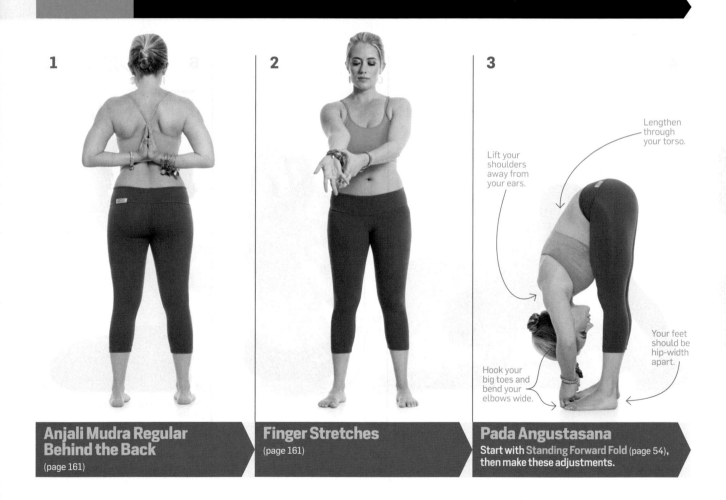

1

Anjali Mudra Regular Behind the Back
(page 161)

2

Finger Stretches
(page 161)

3

Lengthen through your torso.

Lift your shoulders away from your ears.

Hook your big toes and bend your elbows wide.

Your feet should be hip-width apart.

Pada Angustasana
Start with Standing Forward Fold (page 54), then make these adjustments.

Back Pain

I've worked with students ranging

from the young and athletic to the older and mellow, and the most common complaint is back pain. It can stem from overuse or under use, improper posture, or lack of core strength. A 2009 study published in *Alternative Therapies in Health and Medicine* looked at 30 adults with moderate-to-severe chronic lower-back pain. Participants were randomly assigned to a 12-week series of once-weekly hatha yoga classes or put on a waiting list for the class while receiving standard medical care. The yoga group reported a drop in pain scores from an average of 6.7 to 4.4 (where 10 was the worst) after the 12 weeks, while the waiting list group only dropped from 7.5 to 7.1. The yoga group also reported greater reductions in medication use.

These postures will help build strength and flexibility and lessen back pain or even help keep your back pain free. Keep a slight bend in your knees when you work on folding postures, and be careful not to overstretch! Inviting flexibility is always a good idea, but make sure you draw a line between sensation (when you begin to feel tightness in the muscle) and pain (what you feel when you're forcing the stretch too far). If you have a tendency to slump in your chair, prop yourself up on a cushion when you're seated and practice grounding your hips and using your core muscles to sit up straight.

TIP
Add a natural pain reliever such as Arnica—an anti-inflammatory cream or gel made from flowers. Apply before and after your practice, followed by an epsom salt bath.

1

Simple Spinal Twist
(page 109)

2

Relax your forehead and neck.

Walk your arms out straight ahead.

Comfortable Seat Forward Fold
Start with Comfortable Seat (page 93), then make these adjustments.

Jet Lag

You could call me a bit of a jet lag pro.

I am on the road so much I rarely know what time zone I'm in, so I do whatever I can to keep my body happy and healthy. A solid yoga practice is a must when subjecting your body to intense travel. And even if you're on a short flight, it's a good idea to rejuvenate your system with a quick yoga routine once you land on solid ground.

I've chosen these poses bcause they stretch out the muscles that cramp up from sitting for too long and relieve the upper back from poor posture.

TIPS

• Drink lots of water. The air in planes is extremely dry, which can lead to dehydration. It also might help to add an electrolyte tablet to your water.

• Bring a neti pot to clear your nasal passages, which can get congested after flying. (A neti pot is a small contraption, similar to a teapot, that you fill with salt water. You pour the water into one nostril and drain it out the other one to clear your nasal passages.)

• You can also pack melatonin to take before bedtime.

• Lastly, do not nap when you land, no matter how enticing those fluffy hotel pillows look! Get out in the sun, move your body, and do these yoga postures to help restore your natural sleep cycle.

1

Sun Salutation A
(page 44)

Digestion

They say the way to a man's heart is

through his stomach—but I say that applies to anyone! A delicious meal is always a pleasure, but decadent, spicy, or exotic foods can send your tummy into a tizzy. Aside from drinking lots of water and detoxing, yoga is your best bet to calm your system and make amends with a troubled stomach. Twists are fabulous digestion stimulators. They gently massage your internal organs and wring them out just like sponges. Let's do the twist!

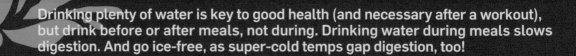

TIP

Drinking plenty of water is key to good health (and necessary after a workout), but drink before or after meals, not during. Drinking water during meals slows digestion. And go ice-free, as super-cold temps gap digestion, too!

1

Make a fist and cover it with your other hand, then place them into your lower belly.

Curl your upper body over your fists and allow them to dig deep.

Child's Pose with Fists at Low Belly Start with Child's Pose (page 149), then make these adjustments.

2

Mountain with Side Stretch (page 67)

3

Half Moon (page 80)

Energy

I think we all suffer from a lack of

energy, whether it's due to stress, lack of sleep, or simply feeling exhausted by a growing to-do list. While yoga can be a restorative act, it can also fire up your system and release massive amounts of energy from within—much healthier (and less expensive) than an extra-large cappuccino with a double shot of espresso!

Kundalini yoga is all about awakening the energy in your spine through movement, repetition, and breath. I talked to Los Angeles teacher Kia Miller, who combines kundalini and vinyasa yoga, about her favorite moves for energy, and she shared this sequence with me. If the holds feel too long, tailor them to your needs and build up to the full holds. The key is to do enough to get your energy flowing and break through whatever has been holding you back. You'll be bounding out of bed in no time!

BREATH OF FIRE

Breath of Fire is a style of breathwork that creates energy from within—and tones your abs, too. Start seated, breathing deeply in and out through your nose. At the top of your inhalation, exhale sharply, releasing all of the air by engaging your diaphragm. As soon as the air is out, inhale sharply and immediately exhale using your diaphragm as a pump. Your breathing should be so fast that the inhalation will happen almost without any thought; the primary focus of this exercise is on making the little punching sensation in your core to help release the breath.

Stretch
Lie on your back and lift your legs and chest about 12 inches off the ground.
Reach your fingers toward your toes and practice Breath of Fire (see opposite) for 2 minutes.

Spine Roll
Pull your knees into your chest and roll back and forth on your spine for 1 minute.

High Heels

Since I was not graced with long legs

or height, I have been forever obsessed with heels. Tall heels. The more treacherous, the better! Ever since I stepped foot into my first pair of platforms, my legs look great, but my feet sometimes feel sore, and my ego is often up in the air. It doesn't matter how gorgeous you look coming out of a chic restaurant in a little black dress and new platforms if you wipe out on the way to the valet. (Trust me, I know!) But don't let this plant fear in your stiletto-loving heart. Follow these simple steps to strengthen and elongate your calves, ankles, and toes. You'll feel confident and balanced at any height.

TIP

After a long night out in heels, sit down and trace the shapes of the alphabet with your feet (using your big toe to "draw"). This relieves both calves and shins. You can also use a foam roller to work out lactic acid and practice Downward Dog to lengthen and release your muscles.

1

Standing Forward Fold with Crossed Legs (page 46)

2

Mountain on Balls of Feet (page 67)

3

Chair on Balls of Feet (page 88)

4

Reclined Big Toe, Part III (page 146)

Yoga for Athletes

*Master these moves for
peak performance*

I adore sports.

I grew up a tomboy and a die-hard University of Kansas Jayhawks fan. Sacrificing my body for a good play came as naturally as breathing—I lived to work up a competitive sweat. I may have since retired my Air Jordans and floor burns, but I still get emotional when I watch the Jayhawks play! I've also become an athlete in my own yogic right. Yoga has taught me to respect my body's abilities and limitations, which is what allows athletes to soar and reach their utmost potential without overdoing it.

Yoga also teaches us how to breathe—something many athletes struggle with, even at elite levels. Practicing breath control helps to strengthen your diaphragm and improve endurance. One of the most important benefits of yoga is that it gives you the ability to prevent new injuries and treat old ones that have accumulated over the years. It's the perfect form of physical therapy to counterbalance the intensity of sports and keep your body strong and supple.

"People always associate yoga with flexibility, but for athletes it means becoming more pliable to make your body more adaptable to stressors. Yoga makes the muscles more like rubber bands and less like guitar strings," says Tiffany Cruikshank, licensed acupuncturist, MAOM, a sports medicine specialist and the yoga teacher at Nike headquarters. She explains that expanding the functional zone of your muscles creates a larger range of contraction that not only helps to prevent injury, but also increases strength and power within the muscles themselves. This means more strength and better performance. Awesome.

Remember: You don't "win" at yoga. Leave your competitive nature on the playing field and don't get caught up in trying to become super flexible right away. "The hardest part about yoga for competitive athletes is that we're so used to giving it our all and pushing ourselves to the limit," Cruikshank notes. You want to reap the benefits of yoga instead of trying to beat them. Be aware of how your body reacts: Sensation is good, but pain is bad. You want pliable muscle tissues, which often means backing off from how far you can actually go. Any pain means you're in the red zone.

Boost Performance with These Routines

Runners and Cyclists

I used to only run if there was a cupcake sale waiting at the end of the 5-K, but have recently fallen in love with running a few times a week. Yoga is the perfect balance to keep your body healthy with running and cycling. Adding a few key yoga poses into your workout will not only strengthen your balance, it will increase body awareness and elongate your muscles, which will in turn lengthen your stride and range of motion. The following poses are great at releasing tension in the hip flexors, hamstrings, glutes, and illiotibial (IT) band, which are used in repetitive motions such as pedaling and striding.

TIP

If you find yourself looking enviously toward another's practice, take a moment to remember that yoga is not about winning or losing! You have no idea what that person is dealing with, what physical blessings they have, or ailments they've overcome. Focusing on your own challenges and accomplishments is what gets you to the finish line.

1

Downward Facing Dog
(page 68)

2

Draw your
shoulders back.

Drop your hips.

Stay on your fingertips.

Crescent Low Lunge Variation
Start with Crescent Low Lunge (page 73),
then make these adjustments.

Tennis

4

Head to Knee
(page 96)

5

Lift your chest.

Keep your top leg's foot in front of the block.

Walk your arms back, keeping them straight.

Sit on a block set at a low or medium height.

Half Reclined Hero Modified on a Block
Start with Hero (page 104), then make these adjustments.

KEEP YOUR EYES ON YOUR OWN MAT

As you broaden your practice and venture out into group classes, remember that practicing yoga with others can be as intimidating as it is inspiring. A class full of limber ballerina types can leave you doubting yourself and wishing your body looked "perfect." When watered with constant doubt, this seed of jealousy can turn into a huge, thorny beast that will shred you from the inside out. It doesn't matter if you're practicing next to Grandma or the lead from *Swan Lake*—what matters is what's happening on your mat. Remembering this will keep your body safe and remind you that there's no need to envy anyone else. A copy will never be as good as the original—so be yourself!

6

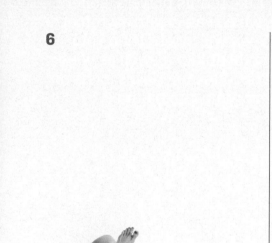

Thread the Needle
(page 108)

7

Simple Spinal Twist
(page 109)

Golf

In golf, everything revolves around the

spine to help the motion of the swing. Like tennis players, golfers often feel repeated impacts on one side, which can create asymmetries in the spine and shoulders over time. Yoga will strengthen your game by reducing stress and increasing flexibility as well as your ability to concentrate on your swing. The following poses focus on the rotator cuffs, spine, and hips, to help maintain balance.

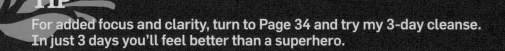

TIP
For added focus and clarity, turn to Page 34 and try my 3-day cleanse.
In just 3 days you'll feel better than a superhero.

1

Keep your hips
over your knees.

Rest on one side of
your face and shoulder.

Press into your palm to
roll open your chest.

Shoulder Thread the Needle
Start with Thread the Needle (page 108), then make these adjustments.

2

Cow Face Arms in Comfortable Seat
Start with Cow Face (page 103), and cross your legs in
Comfortable Seat (page 93).

Golf

3

Lift your opposite leg and arm until they are parallel to the ground.

Keep your bottom arm straight.

Spread your toes.

Gaze forward and down.

4

Cow and Cat with Opposite Arm and Leg Extension
Start with Cow and Cat (page 69), then make these adjustments.

Mountain with Side Stretch
(page 67)

5

6

Revolved Triangle
(page 79)

Cow Face
(page 103)

Soccer

In *Yoga Journal*, Leslie Osborne,

a midfielder for the U.S. Women's National Soccer team, credits her ability to mentally overcome challenges on the field to her yoga practice. Getting over those mental hurdles is just one piece of the puzzle. After all, a soccer player's legs are made for kicking! Practicing yoga will also reinforce your connective tissue around the knees, shins, and ankles, which promotes flexibility in the quads and hamstings. This section's poses focus on improving the health of the hips, quads, hamstrings, and calves to maintain a strong lower body for speed, strength, and endurance.

"The only person you should try to be better than is the person you were yesterday."
—UNKNOWN

MODIFY, MODIFY, MODIFY

Yoga works for everyone because every pose, whether advanced or basic, has a modification.

Think of your yoga practice as a huge puzzle. It's made up of hundreds of pieces that take time to fit together. Sometimes you find the perfect fit right away, and other times you might struggle with a corner or two. I've given you plenty of options for various poses, but feel free to experiment on your own, as well. Don't be afraid to take things down a notch in order to get the right alignment or balance. The pieces won't come together naturally if you force them, so be creative, switch it up, and find what feels good.

1

Downward Facing Dog
(page 68)

2

Extend your top arm until it's straight.

Relax your shoulders.

Rest your hand on your front thigh.

Crescent Low Lunge with Side Stretch Start with Crescent Low Lunge (page 73), then make these adjustments.

Basketball

Former National Basketball Asso-

ciation star Kareem Abdul-Jabbar attributes his remarkably long 20-year basketball career to the benefits he derived from yoga. "I wouldn't have played as long as I had if I hadn't done [yoga]. Basketball is a game of skill, and either you have it or you don't. But being able to maintain the skills is directly related to yoga in my case." All of the jumping and running in basketball requires good knee and hip health to help absorb the impact on the joints. The former Los Angeles Laker star center adds that yoga "really helped my flexibility and range of motion, and it paid off in injuries that I did not get. It also helped me use my strength more efficiently."[1] Focusing on injury prevention, the following poses target the hips, hamstrings, IT band, and spine.

TIP

Create a sweat log. Record everything you do that makes you sweat up to four times a week (every day would be amazing). Whether it's yoga practice, a pickup game, or a long walk, just show up, even if it means waking up an hour earlier than you normally would. Practice discipline and reap the results!

[1] Diane Ballon. "Body and Soul," *Maclean's*, September 19, 1994.

1

2

Cow and Cat
(page 69)

Low Lunge
(page 73)

Swimming and Rowing

Swimming and rowing require repeti-

tive rotational shoulder and hip movements. Adding yoga to your regimen can help you maintain strength and flexibility through your full range of body motion. You'll also develop core strength, and find a comfortable and almost meditative rhythm to your strokes, guided by yogic awareness. The poses in this section focus on stabalizing the rotator cuffs, neutralizing the asymmetries of the spine, and keeping the hips flexible.

REMEMBER

You are unique, talented, and blessed. Your yoga practice is here to guide you and help you overcome your fears and obstacles. Dr. Seuss said it best: "Today you are YOU, that is TRUER than true. There is NO ONE alive who is YOUER than YOU!"

YOGA IS NOT A COMPETITIVE SPORT

The *New York Times* published an article in January 2012 titled "How Yoga Can Wreck Your Body," and it cited case after case of gruesome injuries sustained through yoga practice. Glenn Black, a highly experienced teacher of master classes, said that yoga isn't for the masses and should only be practiced by healthy and strong individuals because the likelihood of someone pushing themselves beyond their limits and causing injury was too strong.

The problem is that, unlike some yogis seems to think, yoga isn't a competitive sport! There are no gold medals handed out for best Triangle or world records bestowed for the longest-held Headstand. Any need to "push" yourself should be motivated by you, and you only.

Glenn Black is also quoted in the article as saying, "Asana is not a panacea or a cure-all. In fact, if you do it with ego or obsession, you'll end up causing problems." Now this I do agree with. This sums it up: Practice without ego. Take your poses to a challenging level while still maintaining a sense of calm and ease. The minute you try to prove something to yourself or others, the yoga is gone and the chance for injury is real.

1

Puppy Dog
(page 156)

2

Cow Face Arms with Strap Start with Cow Face Arms (page 103), but add a strap.

Swimming and Rowing

3

Half Moon with a Block
Start with Half Moon (page 80), then add block.

4

Revolved Triangle with a Block
(page 79)

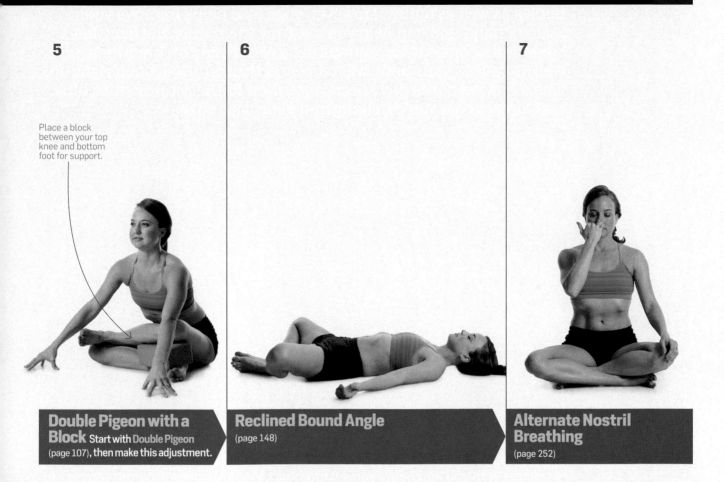

5

Place a block between your top knee and bottom foot for support.

Double Pigeon with a Block Start with Double Pigeon (page 107), **then make this adjustment.**

6

Reclined Bound Angle (page 148)

7

Alternate Nostril Breathing (page 252)

Climbing

Rock climbers need superstrong upper bodies as well as agility. However, yoga also helps improve your state of mind and can help you outgrow the paralyzing fear that sometimes comes when summiting a cliff. Focus on breathing as well as poses—your body will relax and the route will open right up. The following poses pay special attention to the rotator cuffs, hips, and forearms so you can hang and glide with ease.

TIP

Start a manifestation journal. Write down everything that you dream about—your loves, goals, desires. Add photos and anything else that strongly resonates with you and helps you set intention. Visualize your dreams happening, then start living them! Trust that everything happens when the time is right if you are doing your best.

1

Cow Face Arms with Strap
Start with Cow Face Arms (page 103),
but add a strap.

2

Single Pigeon
(page 106)

CHAPTER 9
Yoga for Emotional Health
Moves for maximum mind/body bliss

If only life could be all rainbows

and unicorns—we'd chase the shadows and demons away with pixie dust and optimism! The unfortunate truth is that life isn't always so bright and cheerful. It gets complicated, confusing, and at times even overwhelming. Basically, there's a strong chance that you'll struggle with some kind of depression or emotional issue at some point in your life.

A 2010 *BioPsychoSocial Medicine* article revealed that long-term yoga practice can significantly reduce fear, anger, and fatigue. Researchers administered the Profile of Mood States (POMS) questionnaire to two groups of healthy women— one group of women who had more than 2 years of yoga experience and one group of women who had never practiced yoga. The long-term yoga practitioners had, on average, lower mental disturbance, tension–anxiety, anger–hostility, and fatigue scores than the control group.

Whether you're down in the dumps after being dumped, need motivation to get out of bed and get through the day, or just feel out of sorts emotionally, yoga can help you get back on your feet. Don't despair in times of darkness! I've been there too, and I've found that there's always something valuable to learn, even when all the lights have gone out. Your yoga practice is like a flashlight to illuminate your way out. Use these sequences as helping hands in times of need.

Calming, Mood-Boosting Sequences

Mudras

Strike a pose. Mudras (hand gestures)

can be seen on ancient sculptures and paintings, as well as in modern-day yoga classes and music videos. These beautiful hand gestures go way beyond aesthetics. A mudra is a physical formation used to cultivate a more intense state of mind, and can elevate your practice to a higher level. I've chosen some of the most common and useful to get you started.

TIP

A path with no obstacles often leads to nowhere. Use these mudras to help you through any speed bumps, both in your practice and your life, to get you to a stronger and more knowledgeable place.

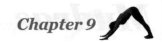

Salutation Mudra (*Anjali Mudra*)

This is the perfect way to start your practice or encourage a meditative state of mind. Salutation Mudra reminds us that all the answers we need are there if we set our intentions.

- Bring your palms together in front of your chest with the thumbs resting lightly on the sternum.
- Press your hands firm and evenly into each other.
- Bow your head slightly and keep the shoulders soft as the chest lifts.

Knowledge Mudra (*Gyana Mudra*)

This mudra helps to discriminate between what is right and wrong. It aids in focus, and sharpens memory and mental concentration.

- Place the tips of your thumbs to the tips of your index fingers.
- Press gently into the pads of your fingers.
- Rotate the palms up if you're looking for energy or help, spin the palms down if you're looking to calm and focus yourself.

Chakras

In yoga, it is believed

that the body contains seven chakras ("wheels," or energy centers). Keeping your chakras open and flowing is important to maintaining a balanced mind-set and energy level. If you practice yoga with the chakras actively in mind, they can help you target any issues you're having and break through energy blockages. I've listed specific poses here that you can use to focus on any of the chakras. You might be surprised by how much better you feel!

● **CROWN CHAKRA:** The highest chakra represents our ability to be fully connected spiritually

LOCATION:	EMOTIONAL ISSUES:	GREAT FOR:	POSES TO PRACTICE: MEDITATION. The crown chakra represents our highest energy. In acupuncture, it's called the "xi" spot and is where all energy stems from. Use your meditation and breath work to envision unity, with all of your chakras working in harmony to keep your system running. Send out a little invitation to health, prosperity, and spirituality. Start small with 5 minutes of meditation and try to work up to 20.
At the very top of the head	Inner or outer beauty, connection to spirituality, pure bliss	People with materialistic urges, spiritual skepticism, or apathy	

● **THIRD-EYE (OR BROW) CHAKRA:** Represents our ability to focus on and see the big picture

LOCATION:	EMOTIONAL ISSUES:	GREAT FOR:	POSES TO PRACTICE: ANY POSTURES WITH YOUR EYES CLOSED. Try balancing in Tree Pose with your eyes closed or standing tall in Mountain while gazing at one point. If you are a true beginner, simply visualize yourself doing beautiful yoga postures even if you've never been able to do them before. This process will tell your body that you can and you will.
On the forehead, above the eyes	Intuition, imagination, wisdom, ability to think and make decisions	People with headaches, nightmares, concentration problems, eye problems, or creativity issues	

● **THROAT CHAKRA:** Represents our ability to communicate

LOCATION:	EMOTIONAL ISSUES:	GREAT FOR:	POSES TO PRACTICE: PLOW, SHOULDER STAND, BRIDGE. These postures help to stretch the neck and open the shoulders to create freedom in this chakra. TIP: Try wearing a turquoise necklace to support this chakra and remain mindful!
In the throat	Communication, expression of feelings or the truth	Smokers, allergy suffers, singers, public speakers, and those who stutter or have thyroid problems	

● **HEART CHAKRA:** Represents our ability to love

LOCATION:	EMOTIONAL ISSUES:	GREAT FOR:	POSES TO PRACTICE: CAMEL, UPWARD FACING BOW, EAGLE POSE, BOW POSE. All of these heart openers or backbends are fantastic for opening the heart. Backbends especially help us build trust and the confidence to truly open up. These poses are fear busters!
Center of chest, just above the heart	Love, joy, inner peace	People who are shy or lonely, have forgiveness issues or breathing issues, or lack love or empathy	

● **SOLAR PLEXUS (OR NAVEL) CHAKRA:** Represents our ability to be confident and in control of our lives

LOCATION:	EMOTIONAL ISSUES:	GREAT FOR:	POSES TO PRACTICE: CROW, HANDSTAND, UPWARD FACING BOW, BOAT. All of these are sensible risk-taking postures. Use them to confront your fears—physical and emotional—and to break through insecurities and increase your confidence.
In the upper abdomen, in the stomach area	Self-worth, self-confidence, self-esteem	People with digestive problems, eating disorders, or low self-esteem and for victims and perfectionists	

● **SACRAL CHAKRA:** Represents our connections with and ability to accept others and new experiences and to accept what is

LOCATION:	EMOTIONAL ISSUES:	GREAT FOR:	POSES TO PRACTICE: COW FACE, BOUND ANGLE, WIDE ANGLE. All hip and groin poses will help to relieve tension and encourage freedom. Instead of forcing these postures, set alignment up and allow yourself to surrender to the pose. Practice long, quiet holds.
In the lower abdomen, about 2 inches below the navel and 2 inches inward	Sense of abundance, well-being, pleasure, sexuality	Workaholics who can't experience pleasure, women experiencing infertility, anyone struggling with sexuality	

● **ROOT CHAKRA:** Represents our foundation and the feeling of being grounded

LOCATION:	EMOTIONAL ISSUES:	GREAT FOR:	POSES TO PRACTICE: STANDING POSES LIKE MOUNTAIN, WARRIOR I, WARRIOR II, REVERSE WARRIOR, AND SIDE ANGLE. RESTORATIVE POSES SUCH AS CHILD'S POSE AND CORPSE. Standing postures will help you to solidify your root and remember how to stand tall and strong. Focus on your feet as the base of your foundation, building your body and all of your energy on top of them. Use the restorative postures to settle an overactive mind and encourage surrender to gravity.
At the base of the spine	Survival issues such as financial independence, money, and food	People who travel too much, have just moved, are newly separated or divorced, or are out of work	

Mild Depression

To this day, I have never left a yoga

class feeling worse than I did before I entered. I can walk into a yoga room wanting to curl up in a ball and by the time I rise from Savasana I feel like a phoenix, resurrected from the ashes of everything that was wearing me out and holding me down. I feel rejuvenated, and, more important, my perspective is refreshed. I've suggested that before you start your yoga routine, you choose an intention, something to focus on during practice. When you're not feeling particularly happy, try to make your intention about joy, and invite it back into your life, pose by pose, breath by breath.

Mild depression can be eased with rejuvenating, playful yoga postures. Poses like Handstand remind you how to feel as carefree as a kid, while backbends are proven to release endorphins. Use this sequence when you're singing the blues. It'll help you pick up the tempo and let your heart sing.

TIP
Start your day with a gratitude practice. As you brush your teeth and get dressed, mentally list all the things that make you happy: your parents, friends, a new outfit, that fabulous meal you had last night. Starting the day remembering your blessings makes you less likely to long for things that you think you lack.

1

Standing Forward Fold
(page 46)

2

Downward Facing Dog
(page 68)

Insomnia

Insomnia—that evil, sleep-stealing

monster that lurks under the bed! It feeds off of stress, anxiety, and what we in yoga call "the constant fluctuations of the mind," or racing thoughts. Tonight, try this sequence to calm your mind, relax your nervous system, and put those pesky sheep-counting nights behind you. Discover the magic of blissful, uninterrupted sleep!

TIPS

• For more restful sleep, try to limit your exposure to light and other stimuli for about an hour before you want to go to sleep. Answering e-mails, surfing the Web, and watching TV all keep your mind firing and make it hard to unwind. Exposure to light slows down your ability to produce melatonin, which helps you fall asleep. If you're sleeping in a room with too much light, invest in an eye mask.

• Rub warm sesame oil on the soles of your feet and into your temples before you go to bed. Sesame oil is known to pacify stress-related symptoms and help you calm your mind.

1

2

Cow and Cat
(page 69)

Seated Forward Fold
(page 95)

Vertigo

4

Warrior II
(page 72)
Hold for 2 minutes on each side.

5

Seated Meditation
(page 329)

6

Corpse (Savasana)
(page 149)

Relaxation

Sequence 1, continued

4

Wide-Leg Forward Fold
(page 84)

5

Seated Forward Fold
(page 95)

6

Bound Angle
(page 102)

7

8

Reclined Bound Angle
(page 146)

Legs Up the Wall
(page 145)

Relaxation

Sequence 2

5

Triangle
(page 78)

6

Half Moon
(page 80)

←

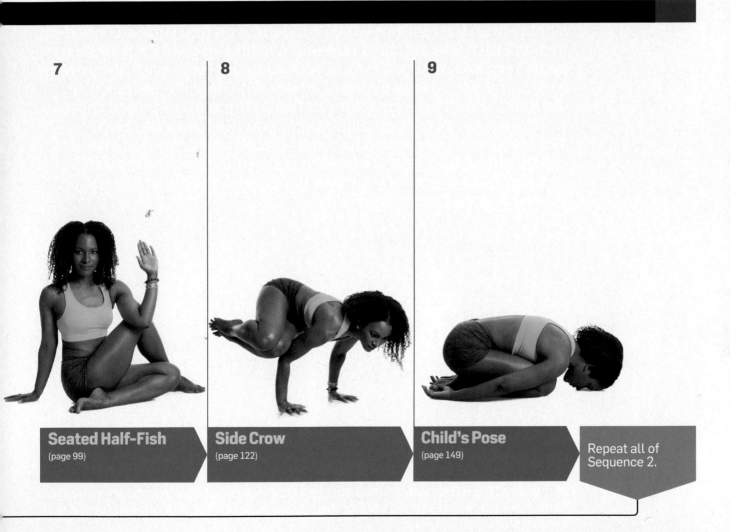

7

Seated Half-Fish
(page 99)

8

Side Crow
(page 122)

9

Child's Pose
(page 149)

Repeat all of
Sequence 2.

Broken Heart

You're in love, blissfully happy, and

singing from the rooftops—then suddenly, you find yourself curled up in a ball with a tearstained face and a feeling of despair. A broken heart very well may be the most painful injury ever—with few proven ways of rehab. There's plenty of advice out there: "Time heals all wounds" and "There are plenty of fish in the sea," but often those words just aren't enough. Sometimes you need tangible help. This sequence is designed to make you feel whole from the inside out. It will rebuild your confidence and remind you that you're completely in charge of your own happiness. Your heart beats for you—and it can never be broken.

TIP

You always have the power to tell yourself that this is not how your story will end. Forget the story and see the soul of the situation. Drop fear and choose love; it will always show you the way.

1

Sun Salutation A
(page 44)

Broken Heart

2

Boat with Bent Knees into Half Boat
Start with Boat with Bent Knees (page 139), then move into Half Boat (page 140).

3

Goddess
(page 157)

M
M
W
pe
ju

m

th

Sl
Lo
yo
co

Fir
Yo
in
int
you
sta
sit
a f
out
in a
you
Re
you
it's

• L
• S
• S
  b
  a
• S

T

Do
to
of
Ro
dis
Ap
co
ing

4

Flying Pigeon
(page 125)

5

Seated Meditation with Palms Over Heart
(page 329)

CHAPTER 10
Yoga and Your Hormones

Balance your body's natural rhythms
and feel good inside and out.

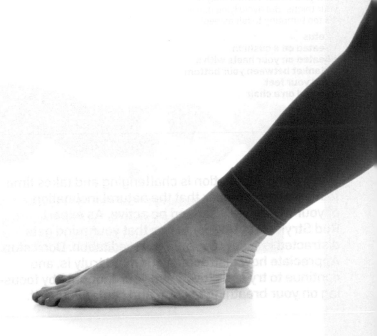

Bloating

4

Supported Bridge with Extended Legs
(page 119)

5

Wind Relieving
Draw your knees into your chest, hip-width apart, and hug tightly.

6

7

Head to Knee
(page 96)

Legs Up the Wall
(page 145)

PMS

This may sound shocking, but when

PMS strikes, sometimes chocolate alone just isn't enough. You can eat yourself into a Ben & Jerry's frenzy, but overindulging on sugar only sharpens the premenstrual pain. The result is a quick upswing in your blood sugar that's followed by a rapid decline—and then your headache and hunger strike again. I know the idea of unrolling your mat isn't nearly as alluring as reaching for the remote to watch reruns of *Sex in the City* is, but do yourself a favor and try this sequence out. Make sure you are equipped with a bolster, if you have one (or use folded blankets). It may take a little extra support to make you feel better, but yoga is up to the challenge. Drop the ice cream and kiss your mood swings good-bye.

TIP

A fellow teacher introduced me to rice-filled pillows that can be warmed up in the microwave or oven and used on any sore part of your body. Try adding the warm pillow to your tummy during some of these restorative poses for extra relaxation.

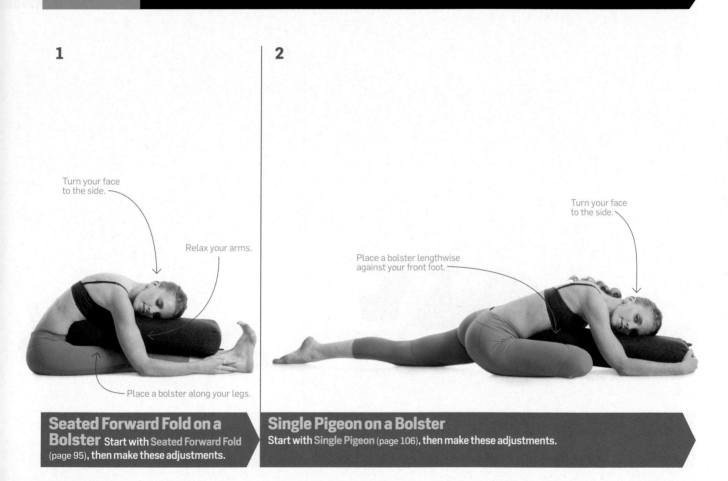

1

Turn your face to the side.

Relax your arms.

Place a bolster along your legs.

Seated Forward Fold on a Bolster Start with Seated Forward Fold (page 95), then make these adjustments.

2

Place a bolster lengthwise against your front foot.

Turn your face to the side.

Single Pigeon on a Bolster
Start with Single Pigeon (page 106), then make these adjustments.

PMS

3

Revolved Bolster Twist Sit sideways at the base of the bolster, bending both knees at a 90-degree angle while keeping the upper thigh in and the lower thigh back. Twist your torso away from your front thigh and rest your face.

4

Supported Reclined Bound Angle
(page 148)

YOGA AND YOUR PERIOD

For years, an epic battle has raged about whether a woman should practice yoga during a woman's menstrual period. Some yoga teachers simply say no inversions should be done. Remember Pattabhi Jois, who pioneered the ashtanga tradition? He encouraged women to take an entire "ladies' holiday" from practice.

Personally, I'm an avid fan of "no flow on my flow," because anything more strenuous than reaching for my Trader Joe's dark chocolate truffle bar is a . . . stretch (in the non-forward-fold sense). Not to mention that bulky pads don't look so cute in skintight Lululemon pants.

I officially consider myself out of commission during the few days leading up to my period, as well as on the first days of my actual period. You can normally find me working flips in a handstand until I can't see straight, but at a certain time of the month I'm usually propped up on the couch with a novel in hand and a spoon poised above a container of Almond Dream chocolate ice cream. On these days, the idea of lifting my frontal hip points to engage my core makes my ovaries scream in surrender—and I'd like to point out that "surrender" is a wonderfully common yogic theme, one I like to teach. I admire the yogis who practice daily no matter what, but even the most devoted practitioner can use a rest.

The whole theory behind taking a break from yoga during your period is, in my mind, a form of respect. Some teachers will say you shouldn't invert during your period because the bloodflow will get stuck. Now, honestly, that sounds like an old wives' tale to me, but logistically speaking, if something is trying to get out, it doesn't make a whole lot of sense to turn it upside down. Or twist it. Or strain it. Or do anything more than easy, supine postures, some bolster snuggling, light walking, and all those bites of chocolate.

But seriously (and I am very serious about my chocolate!), your period should be treated with great respect. It is your body's time to clean and begin a new cycle, much like the full cycles of postures that we go through in yoga. I constantly teach my students to stop and observe themselves before they begin to move. Notice what is happening in your body (as well as your mind) before you race to get where you think you should be.

My advice? If you need a "ladies' holiday," by all means, take one. Don't ignore the way you feel. Stop, observe, acknowledge, respect, and rest. Honestly, you've earned it. Period.

5

Supported Legs Up the Wall
(page 145)

Menopause

I e-mailed an amazing student of mine

who is going through menopause and asked her if any particular yoga poses help to alleviate her symptoms. She replied: "Savasana—lol!" That's not far from the truth! Menopause carries with it an onslaught of frustrating and often painful symptoms—hot flashes, anxiety, irritability, and insomnia, just to name a few. But it's an unavoidable stage of life. Instead of focusing on the dark side, think of it as a rite of passage. In the same way that you should respect your fertile years and menstrual cycles, menopause is a time to honor your body and its natural shift. It always feels better if you and your body are playing for the same team. Once you've made peace (or at least struck a truce!) with your situation, treat yourself to these poses. Instead of giving you a sequence of moves, I've broken down the postures by the symptoms they help.

TIP

An overwhelming number of women claim inversions help the most to relieve their menopausal symptoms. Practice one of the challenging sequences from this book followed by a Handstand and a Headstand, leaving plenty of time to hold the restorative postures. This will help to burn off anxiety and encourage a state of deep rest.

Hot Flashes These unexpected flamethrowers send menopausal women for a major loop. The key to alleviating them is to focus on cooling maneuvers and use plenty of props.

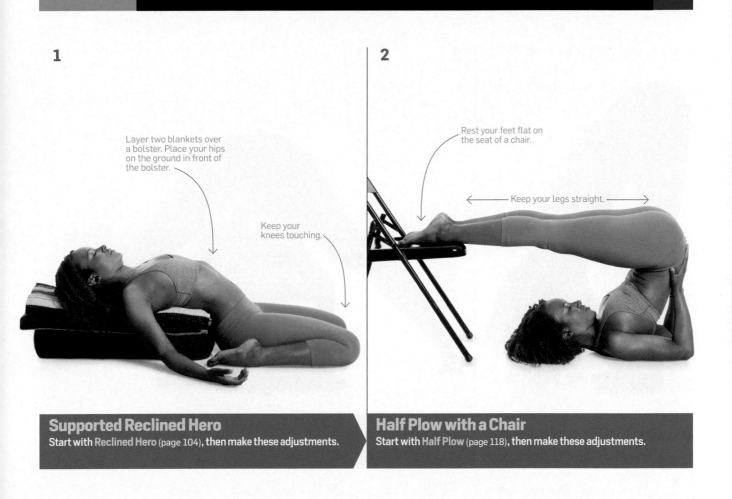

1

Layer two blankets over a bolster. Place your hips on the ground in front of the bolster.

Keep your knees touching.

Supported Reclined Hero
Start with Reclined Hero (page 104), then make these adjustments.

2

Rest your feet flat on the seat of a chair.

Keep your legs straight.

Half Plow with a Chair
Start with Half Plow (page 118), then make these adjustments.

Menopause

Anxiety, Irritability, and Insomnia These poses will help you
shut out distractions, soothe your mind, and calm your nervous system.

1

2

Standing Forward Fold
(page 46)

Wide-Leg Forward Fold
(page 84)

Fatigue This pose opens your chest and heart, delivering a renewed sense of energy and joy!

Supported Bridge
(page 134)

Breakouts and Blemishes

It's impossible to hide breakouts (you can't wear that floppy hat forever), and acne products tend to make matters worse by overdrying your skin and causing peeling and redness. Yoga isn't a dermatologist, but it *can* help to clear impurities from your skin. Inversions increase bloodflow to your face, bringing with it oxygen and other nutrients that fight off free radicals and encourage skin cell renewal. They also leave you with a fresh-faced glow when you're back on your feet.

If you have chronic breakouts, you might want to reconsider your diet. Check out the recipes in Chapter 4 for fresh, nourishing meals. You may even want to detox for a few days to get your system back on track. Complement your healthy eating habits with regular twists that help to eliminate wastes and toxins from your body. Finally, don't forget to work up a sweat! Sweating opens your pores and helps to push toxins out. Make sure you use a good facial cleanser after your practice, and drink plenty of water after practice and in general.

TIPS

• For a natural blemish buster, try dabbing a few drops of tea tree oil or organic coconut oil on your blemishes. Tea tree oil is famous for its drying properties, while coconuts have antifungal and antibacterial properties.

• Nibble on green grapes as a refreshing snack. They are high in vitamin C, magnesium, and potassium, which all help clear your complexion.

• Cheers, mate! Drink several cups of chamomile tea daily as an internal cleanser. It reduces skin inflammation (also in lotions).

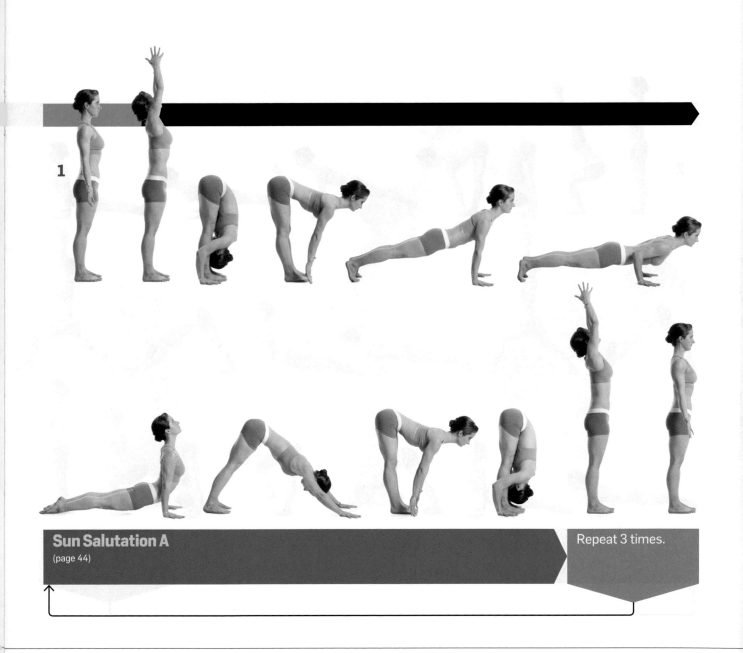

1

Sun Salutation A
(page 44)

Repeat 3 times.

6

7

Revolved Crescent
(page 73)

Repeat on the opposite side starting at step 4.

Dolphin
(page 111)

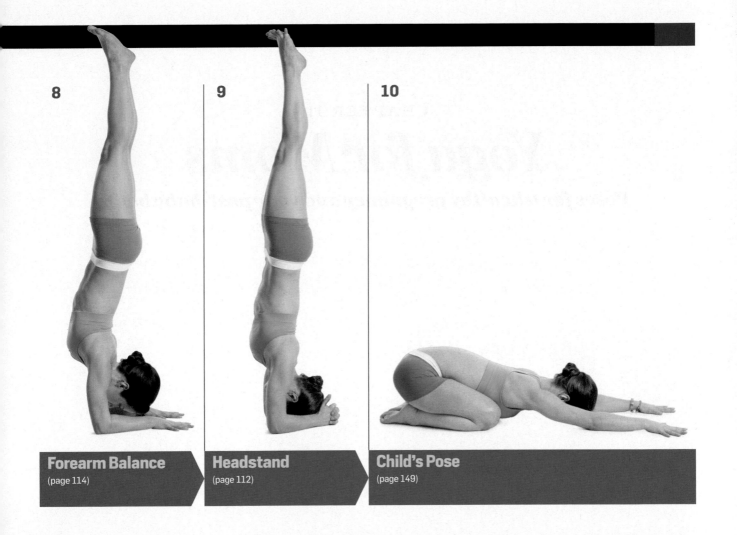

8

Forearm Balance
(page 114)

9

Headstand
(page 112)

10

Child's Pose
(page 149)

Yoga for Moms

Poses for a healthy pregnancy and your post-baby body

Yoga has the ability to

strengthen our bodies, sharpen our minds, and stimulate our souls—but what can it do for a pregnant belly? A 2010 study published in the journal *Quality of Life Research* revealed that, compared with standard prenatal exercises, yoga was significantly more effective at improving the quality of life of pregnant women across the social, psychological, and environmental spectrums.

I couldn't agree with this study more. I see women in all different stages of pregnancy taking classes that range from mellow prenatal routines to sweat-inducing flow sequences. Yoga not only physically relieves women of the aches and pains associated with these 9 months, but it also offers them other amazing benefits—a sense of support, a fun activity, and, most importantly, a way to calm their minds. A high stress level is the worst possible thing for a woman who's expecting, so a regular yoga practice can be exactly what the doctor ordered.

But here's the real reward: Yoga helps with labor! A 2008 study published in *Complementary Therapies in Clinical Practice* found that practicing yoga was an efficient way to improve maternal comfort and decrease pain during labor *and* for 2 hours post-delivery—as well as shorten the length of labor. Sign me up!

Find the level of yoga practice that's comfortable for you and keep at it. Your body and your baby will thank you!

Sequences for the Bump and Beyond

Prenatal

I've worked with plenty of women

who have turned to yoga when they were expecting. My client Giada de Laurentiis was told by her doctor that she couldn't hit the gym after she was about 6 months along. He wanted her to slow down and keep her stress level low. Since she loved to exercise (she had been a gym rat for years), she turned to yoga. I sat down with prenatal and postnatal yoga specialist Heather Seiniger to create the perfect sequence to keep Giada active but relaxed. What we came up with is similar to the sequence Heather contributed in the following pages, and Giada has been hooked since! She, along with countless other mamas-to-be, discovered that yoga helps to keep her chest open, improve her breathing, relax her shoulders, and even increase her leg circulation, which may be reduced by all the additional weight a pregnant woman bears.

Depending on your health history (and your doctor's recommendation), you can keep a fairly strong practice going if you did yoga before you were pregnant. Otherwise, use yoga at your own speed and level of difficulty to feel better and stay calm. I highly recommend practicing every day!

PRENATAL TIPS:

• Keep your feet at least hip-width apart in all standing and seated poses.
• No twisting postures. (If any, keep them incredibly light, focusing on your upper chest.)
• No inverting during your first trimester. If you had a strong inverted practice before your pregnancy you can invert in the second and third trimesters.
• Use only gentle backbends during your third trimester to protect your rectus abdominis.

1

2

Cow and Cat
(page 69)

Opposite Arm–Leg Extension
From Cow and Cat, keep back straight and
extend opposite arm and leg parallel to the ground.

3

4

Rest your forehead
on a blanket.

Child's Pose with Supported Head
Start with Child's Pose (page 149),
then make this adjustment.

Plank or Forearm Plank
(page 141 or 142)

5

Downward Facing Dog
(page 68)

6

Extend
your
heart.

Place your hands onto blocks
at the level of your choice.

Crescent Low Lunge with Blocks
Start with Crescent Low Lunge (page 73),
then make these adjustments.

7

Place your hands onto blocks at a comfortable height.

Warrior III with Blocks
Start with Warrior III (page 74), then make this adjustment.

8

Warrior II
(page 72)

9

Side Angle
(page 76)

10

**Seated Forward Fold
with Strap over Balls of the Feet**
(page 95)

Prenatal

11

Your chest should be slightly extended.

Prop your hips up onto blanket.

Supported Wide Angle Seated Forward Bend
Start with Wide Angle Seated Forward Fold (page 100), **then make these adjustments.**

12

Roll your ribs to the left, then back, to the right, then forward.

Prop your hips up on a blanket.

Bound Angle with Rib Circles
Start with Bound Angle (page 102), **then make these adjustments.**

STRETCH CAREFULLY

Your joints and ligaments may relax and soften as a result of hormones released during pregnancy (relaxin in the third trimester and progesterone from weeks 28 through 30). This means you'll be much more flexible than normal. But I recommend doing postures at about 70% percent of your capability. Even if it feels good to go deep, back off just a bit. It's better to keep your body strong than to overstretch it. (Think of an overstretched rubber band: . . . no es bueno!)

KEEP CALM AND COOL

Keep your breath flowing and easy, and emphasize your exhalations—doing so can be cooling and calming. If you find yourself overheating, keep your arms down and exhale through your mouth.

13

Corpse (Savasana) with Bolster
Start with Corpse (page 149), but add a bolster.

Mommy and Me

Feel like you don't have any time to do
yoga? No worries—bring baby along! You can incorporate your baby into your yoga routine, which will keeping everyone laughing and smiling as you sweat and shed your baby weight! Here's a sequence of poses that will help get you back into your practice and keep your little one occupied at the same time.

TIPS

• Ease back into exercise gradually, to avoid injury. Also, remember to keep your chest open and your shoulders down, as they tend to close and tighten from nursing and carrying your baby.

• For added strength-building, take walks with your baby carried against the front of your body in a sling or carrier. They'll love being close to you, and you'll love shedding extra pounds from the workout.

1

Keep your knees bent and your shins parallel to the ground.

Boat
(page 139)

2

Let your little one sit on your belly as you engage your core and legs.

Leg Lowers
Use your baby to engage your core and lengthen your tailbone.

Mommy and Me

3

Relax your shoulders and bend your elbows.

Keep a slight bend in your knees.

Bend deeper as you lift your little one higher!

Keep your weight in your heels.

Chair
(page 88)

4

Encourage your little one to crawl through the tunnel!

Downward Facing Dog
(page 68)

Giselle MARI

Giselle Mari is an advanced certified jivamukti yoga teacher whose yogic path began in the early '90s. Being a bit of a wild child, she was drawn to the jivamukti yoga method early on and began her extensive study with her gurus Sharon Gannon and David Life, both of whom she has joyfully assisted throughout the western United States.

Yoga has shown Giselle that the inflexibility in the body is secondary to the inflexibility of the mind. She is reminded every day that her body is a vehicle for her highest self and, like any protective case for

> "The practice of yoga is both revealing and challenging—it can shine a light on the dark corners of your being: physically, mentally, energetically, and spiritually. Like any good relationship, the practice keeps you on your toes and can humble you quickly."

something valuable, she wants to take care of it while she has it! Her favorite yoga poses are twists and inversions because they literally change your perspective of the world and ask you to see both sides of what is being presented.

Giselle is based in the San Francisco Bay area and currently teaches dynamic and insightful classes and workshops at yoga conferences and festivals in the United States as well as around the globe. She has been featured in Yoga Journal and Yoga International and has had the honor of appearing on their covers as well. For more information visit funkyjiva.com.

CHAPTER 12

Yoga for Sex

**Radiate confidence with routines
that take you from the mat to the sack**

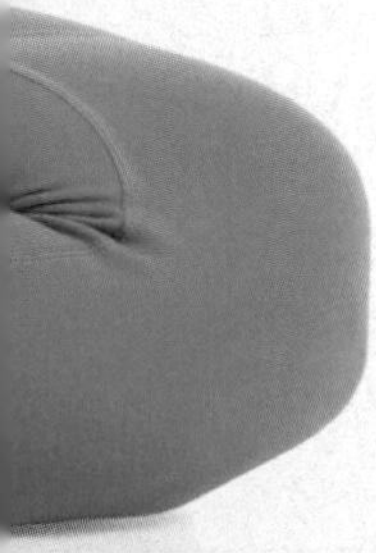

That's right, I said "sex."

You've made it through the essential yoga poses and routines. You've altered your diet to help you be healthy and aware. You've mastered some poses and even have some sequences that you practice on a regular basis, and you feel slimmer, fitter, and more mentally balanced. You have officially graduated to the good stuff. It's time to learn how yoga will rock your sex life! A 2010 study published in the *Journal of Sexual Medicine* found that yoga was effective in improving women's desire, arousal, lubrication, orgasm, and sexual satisfaction, and in lessening sexual pain.

Yoga is the total trifecta: It unifies and improves the body, mind, and soul. Sex (or, I should say, really satisfying sex) is also a combination of all three.

First of all, it's about having a strong physical connection with your partner. Sexual desire often boils down to instinctual, primal attraction. Once those pheromones kick in, bam—it's time to communicate without words. But in addition to getting turned on by the sight of hot, rock-hard abs, truly great sex requires a mindfulness that goes deeper than the layer of touchable skin. One-night stands can feel thrilling and risqué, but a meaningful mind–body connection builds trust, which leads to safe sexual exploration. You'll have the confidence to tell your partner what you like and don't like. You'll feel encouraged to try new things, or simply to enjoy the simplicity of the tried and true.

Once you have physical attraction and a deeper connection, you can dive into spirituality. A spiritual sexual connection takes you to a level where you and your partner share the same energy, even though you're in different bodies—you truly become one, as they say. This takes sex beyond a physical act and into one of the deepest and purest ways to connect and share yourself with another person. It's both pleasurable and meaningful, and yoga can help get you there.

Better Sex Sequences

OM-GASM

The French had it right when they nicknamed the orgasm *la petite mort*, or "the little death." Orgasm is a transcendent moment when the body loses all control—the stars align, poetry becomes the common tongue, and spirituality doesn't even require a second thought. There is a burst of "life force," which is referred to as "prana" in yoga. The life force bursts out of our physical bodies, causing a brief death—a complete surrender, if you will.

The feeling of orgasm is comparable only to that perfect salted caramel *pot de crème* or the butterfly feeling in your stomach when you first fall head over heels—it exemplifies love. Unfortunately, this amazing experience is often searched for in vain. There are many reasons why orgasms can be elusive, among them a lack of trust, comfort, surrender, breath, or even body awareness. Yoga tackles all of these subjects in the hope that you'll reach spiritual enlightenment on and off the mat. (Yes, I mean in bed!) The practice of breath control (pranayama) enables you to live in the moment. It slows down your mind, curbs distraction, and allows you to concentrate on the subject at hand—pleasure.

Try this partner breathing routine to calm your mind and instantly connect with your partner.

Partner Breathing
Assume Buddha Straddle in the buff with your partner. Come into a soft embrace and close your eyes. Begin focusing on your breath, breathing in and out through your mouths. Once you are comfortable with your own breath, begin to sync it with your partner's. As one of you exhales, the other inhales their breath, and vice versa. Once you hit a rhythm doing this, begin to work the pelvis. As you inhale, arch your lower back. Exhale as you thrust your pelvis toward your partner. Continue breathing as you link your hips without penetration.

Meditate on the Big 'O'
Often, people who have difficulty climaxing are those who find it impossible to clear their minds. The best thing you can do for your libido is to meditate. Close your eyes and slow down your breathing. Once your breathing has calmed, exhale all of the air from your lungs in one quick breath. Inhale for a slow count of 4. Exhale for 2 counts. Repeat this cycle 3 to 5 times. Now you're ready to get it on!

Confidence, Energy, and Endurance

Nothing's sexier than a confident

partner. You can do squats till you can bounce a quarter off your butt, but if you don't believe you're sexy, it won't translate to someone else. Practicing yoga blends the physical bonus of gaining strength and an attractive figure with the confidence that your body type is perfect and made just for you.

Once you truly believe you're a sex goddess (because yeah—you are!), it's time to jump-start Yoga Sex Boot Camp. You've got the attitude, now it's time to train. Postures that strengthen your lower back will improve your ability to move and thrust without cramping or fatigue. Hip-opening postures increase the blood flood (hello, orgasm buddy!) and allow for a greater range of motion. Core strengtheners help you to sit, swing, and bounce longer and stronger. Put simply: More yoga equals more energy, which equals more (and better) sex!

Here's a list of postures that can help to make your playtime last longer and be way more exciting.

INDIVIDUAL POSES

Men

1

Garland
(page 70)

2

Bound Angle
(page 102)

Confidence, Energy, and Endurance

Men

3

Plank
(page 141)

4

Locust
(page 131)

Women

1

Happy Baby
(page 108)

2

**Wide Angle
Seated Forward Bend**
(page 100)

Confidence, Energy, and Endurance

Women

3

Half Moon
(page 80)

4

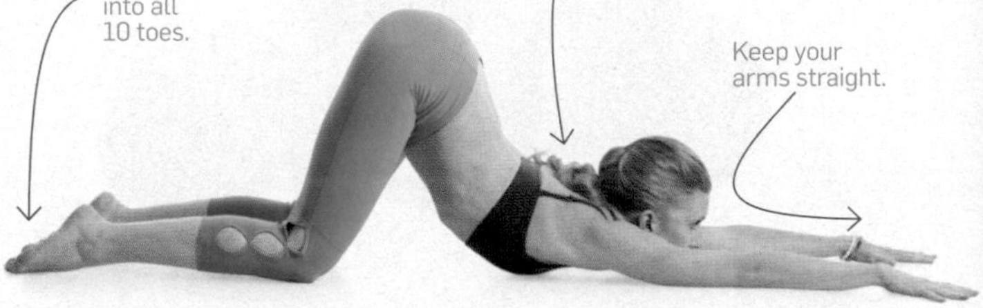

Press down into all 10 toes.

Melt your chest and throat toward the ground.

Keep your arms straight.

Puppy Dog Stretch
Start with Puppy Dog (page 156), then make these adjustments.

Mary Clare SWEET

Mary Clare's parents introduced her to meditation at a very young age. As she grew up she started practicing yoga as a complement to her ballet and jazz classes. After struggling in her teenage years, she uncovered the secret of the yoga practice when she was in her twenties and began to fall in love with her life.

The practice of yoga has so much diversity that anything is truly possible; that coupled with this idea that we all have the same capacity for love, evolution, and experience is just one of the reasons that Mary Clare practices yoga. It also makes her feel strong and centered. Having a tendency to daydream and float off into outer space, she says the asanas keep her grounded in the present moment—where the past can't hold her back and the future holds limitless possibilities.

The physical practice keeps our bodies in great shape but the mental practice is just as important. Mary Clare credits her positive disposition to the time she spends meditating in gratitude. She feels that when you focus on abundance, you invite more of what you want into your life than when you focus on the negative. She even attributes her good health and confident body image to yoga. She used to

> "I rarely get sick, I am awake in the morning and tired at night, I never have back or joint pain, and I experience a high level of clarity. Because my mind and body connection is strong and clear, I can honor little red flags my immune system sends my way. I feel like all systems run well because of my consistent yoga practice."

see her body as something that needed fixing. Now she simply checks in with her body to understand how she can serve it more effectively.

Mary Clare owns Lotus House of Yoga, a vinyasa studio in Omaha, Nebraska. The classes she leads are fun, challenging, and filled with love.

Intimacy and Sensuality

Maybe you brought sexy back, but

you still can't quite get on the same track as your partner. Broken lines of communication make it almost impossible to sync up in bed. We're all living different, busy lives that don't always mesh at home. You can sit there and talk it out until you're blue in the face, but often a good shared yoga session is all you need. It helps to "speak" a language that transcends careers and opinions to find a way to reconnect.

When words fail you, unroll your yoga mats and practice moving and breathing together. Your heart rates will rise for long enough for you to sweat out stress and then lower again to calm your hearts (just in time to send those pulses racing again!). Yoga will help you to clear your minds and find what keeps you intertwined. Not to mention that breathing and sweating together is pretty compelling foreplay. Be playful, explore each other's rhythms and bodies, and know that simply being in close contact with one another's hearts can be extremely healing and enticing.

TIP

The simplicity of not talking (or nagging) and instead merely syncing your breath with your lover's is a potent tool. The lack of visual cues and reliance on connection through touch and breathing will start to unify your two bodies for the ultimate act of unification.

LOVERS' LOCK

One of my favorite T-shirts of all time reads: Mula Bandha Is for Lovers.

This makes me a bona fide yoga dork, but it is rather clever. If you remember from page 14, the mula bandha is the root lock located between the anus and genitals. This is where the pubo-coccygeal (PC) muscle lies. We engage this lock during yoga practice when we want to lift our body weight up or get that extra bit of "zip" to feel light in a pose. Activating this muscle is often described as making the motion of holding back from urinating. The PC muscle is located deep within the pelvis. It is directly connected to the genitalia, which means that it helps control the strength of and bloodflow to this area.

Toning your PC muscle increases pleasure, performance, and sensation. It also can intensify your orgasms and give you the strength to solidly grip your man—giving him a memorable experience as well! Mastering these muscles can get you one step closer to the elusive "minigasm" that is often a precursor to the real deal. That means longer love-making and, maybe, a very happy and joyous moment when you climax together.

1

Close your eyes.

Rest your palms facing upward.

Seated Meditation Bond

Sit in Comfortable Seat (page 93), with your backs pressed together. Sit up tall, gently pressing into each other's body and back of your head. Rest your palms facing upward in your lap. Close your eyes and sync your breath, breathing slow, deep, and full inhales and exhales.

2

Sit tall with your backs pressed together.

Revolve your chest to the right.

Seated Inner-Thigh Twist

Sit tall with your backs pressed together and reach your right arm towards their left thigh and your left arm onto your right thigh. Gently press down on the thigh or slide your hand to their inner thigh. Push your legs down with your hand as you sit tall and revolve your chest to the right. Repeat on the other side.

Intimacy and Sensuality

3

Press hips into the ground.

Lift your chest.

Pull gently to keep chest open.

Seated Partner Twist

Sit in either Comfortable Seat (page 93) or Lotus (page 329) facing each other, with your knees touching. Take your right arm behind your back and reach your hand toward your hip. Extend your left arm forward as you spiral your chest toward the right to grab your partner's right hand. Gently pull on each other's arms.

4

Close your eyes, lightly press the center of your brows together and sync your breathing.

Cross your ankles.

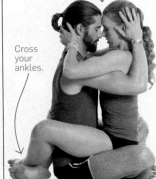

Buddha Straddle

Place yourself onto your partner's lap facing him. Wrap your legs around his torso and bring your palms to both sides of each other's heads.

5

Engage your lower belly.

Root your hips down.

Relax your throat.

Buddha Bliss

Sit in Buddha Straddle and grab each other's forearms (or above the elbows). Root your hips down and engage your lower belly. Inhale deeply and lift your chest, then exhale, and lean back. Arch your chests and bring your arms to straight continuing to hold onto each other.

6

YOGA SEX POSITIONS

Okay, time to stop (really, I mean "start") fooling around. You have the tools you need to get aroused, stay there, and be strong. Now it's time to put these efforts to the test! Unravel some of your favorite yoga poses in your bedroom for creative sexual playtime. And have fun! No one's handing out gold stars at the end of the night. Be creative, breathe, and get down and dirty in your Downward Facing Dog.

Child's Play

WOMAN: Come into **Child's Pose** (page 149) with your hips slightly elevated above your heels. Rest your forehead on something soft on the floor and stretch your arms straight out in front of you.

MAN: Come into a wide squat behind your woman and enter her from behind. Hold on to her shoulders for leverage to go deeper.

Route 69 Overpass

WOMAN: Straddle your man's head, facing toward his feet. Place your hands under his hips to help him lift his pelvis as you pleasure him orally.

MAN: Come into **Bridge** (page 134) with your arms alongside your body.

Tunnel Bridge

WOMAN: Come into **Bridge** (page 134).

MAN: Kneel between your woman's legs, holding up her hips. Enter her, keeping her hips elevated.

Happy, Baby!

WOMAN: Come into **Happy Baby** (page 108). Lightly lift your hips or place a pillow beneath your lower back for support.

MAN: Kneel facing your woman and enter her while holding her feet. Gently press down to root her hips.

Downward Doggie Style

WOMAN: Come into **Downward Facing Dog** (page 68) (you may need to adjust your stance according to your partner's height).

MAN: Stand behind your woman with your feet spread wide beyond hers. Enter her from behind, rolling your chest over her with your arms caressing her back or standing tall and holding the creases of her hips.

Plow the Field

WOMAN: Come into a modified **Plow** (page 118) by lifting your legs straight into the air. Hold on to your calves or ankles and gently draw your legs back so that your hips lift slightly.

MAN: Come into **Plank** (page 141) with your hands on either side of your woman's torso. Enter her from this position, rocking slowly back and forth.

Reach toward your partners lower back.

Loving Embrace

Come into Bound Angle (page 102). Have your partner come into a wide legged Seated Forward Fold with the soles of his feet pressing into your ankles. Walk your arms and chest forward holding onto his thighs. Your partner should fold gently over your head and upper back to rest his arms on your lower back or hold your hips. Switch roles and repeat.

Intimacy and Sensuality

7

Plant your hips into the ground.

8

Extend your chest forward and up as you lean against his back.

Gently press down.

Digging for Diamonds

Start in Wide Angle Seated Forward Bend (page 100), facing one another. Press the outer edges of your heels into each other's foot or inside of foot. Grab hold of each other's forearms. One person should lean back as the other plants their hips into the ground and extends their chest forward with a flat back. Switch roles and repeat. Talk to each other about what feels good—when to go deeper and when to back off.

Bound Blanket

Have your partner start in Bound Angle Pose (page 102). Come onto your knees behind your partner. Wrap your knees around his hips to help secure them into the ground. Place your palms onto his upper thighs. Switch roles and repeat.

9

Relax your
neck and close
your eyes.

Pretzel Savasana

Have your partner lie on his back with his legs spread hip width apart. Sit facing your partner directly in front
of his pelvis and drape your legs over his hips so that your feet rest along the sides of his chest. Lie back
and rest for 5 minutes. Afterward, massage each other's feet, then help each other up into a seated embrace.

CHAPTER 13

Yoga for Life

Everything you need to take it to the next level

J

ust like little birdies need to leave the nest to learn how to fly, you'll eventually want to venture beyond these pages to expand your yoga experience. There are plenty of sequences here in the book to work on, but the real (and very big) world of yoga holds a multitude of opportunities. Get excited! You're ready to explore even more beautiful twists and turns (and splits and inversions) that will keep you challenged, intrigued, calm, and smiling.

Yoga for Life

A home practice is a fabulous thing, but nothing compares to the energy of a public class and the well-trained eye of an instructor to watch your alignment. I highly recommend finding a local studio with an experienced teacher to help you along your path. He or she can answer your questions and, with your classmates, provide a supportive community. (My yoga buddies often become like extended family!)

If you're not quite ready to fall out of the nest yet or there's no nearby studio, check out great online resources like yogajournal.com and yogaglo.com. YogaGlo offers classes of varying lengths, levels, and styles, and they're new every day via streaming video. And it's cheap! An unlimited subscription to YogaGlo costs $18 a month, whereas many yoga classes cost that much per session. If money isn't an issue, consider hiring a teacher for a few private sessions to help build your confidence and awareness.

If you're lucky enough to have a yoga studio on every block, you'll want to do a bit of research to find out which one is right for you. Ask around and check out online reviews on sites like yelp.com. Pop in to experience the vibe and see how comfortable you feel there. It's ideal to find a studio close to home so you can walk or bike there—no excuses! And don't be afraid to try out different studios and teachers before you make a commitment. I did not like my first class experience because the teacher gave me the heebie-jeebies. I was ready to write yoga off completely until my friend dragged me to a different class—with a teacher I absolutely adored. Don't judge yoga itself by the teacher or class; keep exploring until you find a match. Trust me—it's out there.

What's Your Yoga Type?

The best answer to this is, really, whatever you please at any given moment! Don't feel that you need to stick to a specific style of yoga. It can be educational and entertaining to explore them all. That being said, you will find a style that you prefer, so I've created an overview of the main styles to help you identify them.

TIP: If you're on a budget, consider looking for special deals to pay for yoga classes. Many studios offer less expensive community classes in the middle of the day. Others exchange free classes for work (like manning the front desk or helping to clean or organize the studio). Ask the people at the front desk for options for financial help. Chances are they'll welcome the idea and figure out a way to keep you on your mat.

Yoga Etiquette

Once you're ready to join a group, here are a few tips to keep in mind so you can get the most out of your practice!

HYDRATE BEFORE SHOWING UP

Many classes these days tend to be packed and hot. You'll want to bring a water bottle to class, but many teachers won't allow it because it disrupts the tapas (or heat) and discipline building. Plus, you don't want water swishing around in

ANANDA

| DESCRIPTION: Gentle poses that focus on meditation | IDEAL FOR: Beginners who want to ease into the practice or slow down and do more meditation | OM FACTOR: Chanting at the beginning and end of class | PHYSICAL DIFFICULTY: LOW |

ANUSARA

| DESCRIPTION: Geared toward heart-opening backbends with a deep focus on postures | IDEAL FOR: Those looking for a playful, loving community | OM FACTOR: Invocation chant with harmonium accompaniment at the beginning and end of class, with stories woven in | PHYSICAL DIFFICULTY: MEDIUM TO HIGH |

ASHTANGA

| DESCRIPTION: An athletic "flow" style that combines fast-paced movement with breathwork | IDEAL FOR: Type A people who are driven and dedicated, and those who want an intense practice that will have visible results | OM FACTOR: Usually a lengthy but very straight-forward chant at the beginning and end of class | PHYSICAL DIFFICULTY: HIGH |

BIKRAM

| DESCRIPTION: Uses the same 26-posture series each time, but it's done in a 105°F room. You will sweat! | IDEAL FOR: Sweat junkies who aren't afraid of intense heat | OM FACTOR: No chanting | PHYSICAL DIFFICULTY: HIGH |

HATHA

| DESCRIPTION: A generic term used to describe any form of yoga that includes asanas (poses) | IDEAL FOR: Those who are unsure about which class to take and want a general introduction | OM FACTOR: Depends on the teacher | PHYSICAL DIFFICULTY: MEDIUM TO HIGH |

IYENGAR

| DESCRIPTION: Poses are held for longer than usual with a focus on alignment | IDEAL FOR: Teacher trainees, those who want to improve their alignment, and those with injuries | OM FACTOR: Depends on the teacher | PHYSICAL DIFFICULTY: MEDIUM TO HIGH |

KUNDALINI

| DESCRIPTION: Primarily seated positions combined with breathing and movement techniques | IDEAL FOR: Those who want to stimulate energy, focus, and deep meditation | OM FACTOR: Lots of chanting at the beginning and end of class with deep meditation and energy work | PHYSICAL DIFFICULTY: MEDIUM |

POWER

| DESCRIPTION: A vigorous workout that moves quickly through a series of linked poses and generates lots of sweat and physical release | IDEAL FOR: Athletes and those driven to work out | OM FACTOR: Depends on the teacher | PHYSICAL DIFFICULTY: HIGH |

VINYASA

| DESCRIPTION: A series of athletic poses combining movement with breathwork | IDEAL FOR: Those who want a good workout that often is set to music | OM FACTOR: Usually a brief chant or om at the beginning and end of class | PHYSICAL DIFFICULTY: MEDIUM TO HIGH |

your belly as you twist and flip upside down. Make sure to hydrate before you enter the class so you'll work up a good sweat. You can replenish afterward. Exception: If you're taking a Bikram yoga class (which is usually held in a room heated to 105°F or higher), bring water, without a doubt.

SAVE DINNER FOR LATER

I made the mistake of eating a big bowl of pasta (and wearing jean shorts!) to my very first yoga class. Not only did my denim outfit truly suck when it got soaked with sweat, my tummy also was not happy with me during the class. It's amazing how disruptive even a small amount of food can be during a yoga sequence. Eat something light (fruit, a protein bar, or almond butter on whole wheat bread) about 2 hours before class. It will make your practice—and your next meal—that much more enjoyable.

ARRIVE EARLY

If it's your first time at a studio, you'll likely be asked to fill out a waiver or other paperwork, so make sure you have a few extra minutes to handle that business and also get yourself settled. Depending on the popularity of the teacher, many classes will sell out, so give yourself time to show up, sign in, and find a space in the room before the stampede. In general, it's nice to have some alone time on your mat before class to slow down and transition from regular life to your practice.

SPEAK UP

If you have any injuries, tell the teacher! Grab them before class or gently wave them over during class to let them know. It's perfectly fine to say that you don't want physical adjustments because something hurts or is bothering you, or that you might need modifications to help certain areas of your body. Just be open and respectful, of both the teacher and yourself.

NO PHONES ALLOWED

Seriously. Putting your phone on vibrate or mute does not count. Just make it a habit to leave your phone, iPod, pager, BlackBerry, and any other devices in the car or in your locker—anywhere that's not the yoga room. No matter how hard you try, you will forget one day and be that person whose phone starts ringing while everyone is lying peacefully in Savasana! It's a surefire way to whip you out of a calm place, as well as to get nasty looks from the teacher and other students. Let yoga class be your time to disconnect from the outside world.

SHOES OFF

Most yoga studios have cubbies outside the room to place your shoes in, so make sure you leave them there. No shoes keeps the studio clean (you put your mat, hands, and face on that floor) and also just shows respect. If you're worried about someone taking your designer heels, bag them and place them in the back of the room—just don't come stomping in with them on!

GRAB YOUR PROPS

If you think you'll want a strap, blocks, or a blanket, grab them at the beginning of class. This will prevent you from having to walk around the maze of students in the middle of a limb-weaving sequence and give you options for modifications for all poses. Remember, using props doesn't make the pose "easier" or make you look dorky—it makes yoga better for your body. Always choose the variation that makes you feel best.

LATE ARRIVAL

Some studios won't let you in the yoga room after a certain amount of the class is over. If you do find yourself running late (it happens to the best of us), wait until the opening meditation is finished to enter. Most rooms have peepholes or a window to look in. When you enter, take care to avoid slamming your mat down or tossing your keys and bag to the floor. Come in quietly and find a space. It's totally fine to ask someone to move over to make space for you—just be kind.

TAKE TIME TO REST

Life is busy, but take the 5 minutes at the end of class to rest in Savasana. Yoga isn't about building up a sweat and then racing for the hills once the pace slows down. Yoga is all about balance—uniting your strength and surrender. If you know you'll need to leave class early, make sure to do so before Savasana, and plan accordingly so you don't disrupt everyone when you leave. If you can stay, though, taking the time to do Savasana is often the ticket to feeling truly renewed when you leave the class. Try bringing an eye pillow to help you relax and move into your own world for just 5 minutes. Enjoy and rest.

Yoga Couture

Technically, you can wear whatever you want to for yoga. The golden rule is to be comfortable, but you should avoid baggy clothing because you'll just end up getting caught up in your own shirt or tripping on your sweatpants. I advise wearing something with spandex so the teacher can see your alignment. Most importantly, wear something that you feel good in. You don't want to have to fuss with your clothes while you practice.

Part of my job is being in the public eye. From writing regular blog posts and articles to teaching weekly online at yogaglo.com, I'm seen all the time. And just like any fashionista, I, too, face the dreaded question: "What should I wear?" Clearly, yoga isn't about brands or what style pants you're wearing, but it can certainly be fun and expressive! Wearing the same black leggings and top every day might be flattering, but nothing lifts my spirits like unique, colorful clothing.

I often receive e-mails with comments like, "Where did you get those great pants?!" so I thought I'd share my favorite brands and shops. Happy shopping!

ALTERNATIVE APPAREL

This awesome company is super hip and eco-friendly, and its clothes come in a wide array of colors, cuts, and options.

POSES FOR PAWS

I co-created the charity Poses for Paws in 2008 to repay the love that animals have brought into my life (my beloved puggle, Ashi, has been my companion for 6 years). Poses for Paws chooses a different animal shelter or organization to raise money for each year. We host yoga events and team up with companies like ToeSox and Tiny Devotions to support these shelters and our overall mission of helping and healing animals in need. For more information, visit www.posesforpaws.com, or follow us on Facebook.

Yoga for Life

They offer great transitional clothes if you're not into hardcore yoga gear. Their lines are studio and street friendly, so you can ease into your Downward Facing Dog as easily as you slip into your cute boots and shawl on the way out of class.
alternativeapparel.com

LULULEMON
This quirky Canadian company has taken the states by storm. With more than 140 stores nationwide and a major online presence, it's easy to see why it has become a staple store for yogis. It's famous for its Groove Pant, which makes anyone's derriere look superb! They also offer flattering tops, cover-ups, jackets, and hoodies, as well as a great line for men.
lululemon.com

ELISABETTA ROGIANI
This sassy Los Angeles–based Italian wants to make you look sexy. Her tights are my all-time favorites—they're incredibly flattering (never cutting into your passion handles) and come in all colors of the rainbow. Her fabric feels like butter and you often get a personal phone call from her when you order. Just be prepared to chat for a while. Ciao, darling!
rogiani.com

BEYOND YOGA
This line is elegant and flattering on all body types. I've even seen 80-year-old women rocking its gear! The styles embrace a woman's body and the fabric is deliciously soft. The company also offers seasonal lines with bold, playful colors for spring/summer and rich, darker colors for fall/winter.
iambeyond.com

HARD TAIL FOREVER
This California company is based in Santa Monica, where it has a store you could get lost in for hours, browsing the racks of great styles with edgy cuts and fun patterns. If you're not in SoCal, you can often find its lines at yoga studios or in larger department stores like Nordstrom and Bloomingdale's. Hard Tail offers both yoga and lifestyle clothing for the fashion-conscious yogi.
hardtailforever.com

CHASER
This rocker T-shirt company focuses on soft, flowing shirts with prints from bands like Pink Floyd and Journey. I love to use them as cover-ups on the way to the studio, and they look just as cute over jeans on my way out of class.
chaserbrand.com

TEEKI
This amazing company makes fashion sustainable. All of their products—yoga clothing and bikinis—are made out of recycled water bottles! The cuts are comfortable, flattering and their patterns are complete show-stoppers. Just be prepared for plenty of longing looks and conversations when you wear their line!
teeki.com

KIRAGRACE

This gorgeous line was created by Kira Karmazin, who also developed successful product lines for Lucy Activewear, Victoria's Secret, and Gap. She created an amazing Goddess Collection that brings out women's inner beauty and strength. Her unique and accessible designs are absolute favorites of mine. *kiragrace.com*

More Yoga Resources

GAIAM

You can find pretty much anything you need here—mats, props, fitness gear, clothing, and even yoga DVDs (yup, including mine). It's a good one-stop shop. You can find many of its products at most Whole Foods Markets, as well. *gaiam.com*

MANDUKA

These guys make the Cadillac of yoga mats. Their Black Mat PRO is a monster (almost 10 pounds for the 85-inch mat!), but it will last for the rest of your life. They also have a great line of eco-friendly mats, as well as props and bags. *manduka.com*

YOGITOES

This eco-friendly and innovative Santa Monica company is always on the cutting edge. Owner Susan Nichols perfected the skidless towel to put on your mat, and you'll now see it at yoga studios worldwide. The Skidless is perfect for any yogi who loves to sweat. The company also created a stretch yoga strap—the Strap Stretch—that is incredibly helpful when learning inversions, arm balances, and any pose where you need more shoulder support. *yogitoes.com*

TOESOX

These adorable skidless socks with separate toes can be found in Pilates and yoga studios across the globe. The tiny San Diego–based company that makes them also believes in giving back. I've had the honor of being this company's ambassador for years, and I partnered with it to create Hot Pink ToeSox to benefit Poses for Paws (my personal project to raise money for animal shelters), as well as socks to help raise breast cancer awareness. There's nothing like knowing you're helping others as well as yourself! *toesox.com*

Index

Underscored page references indicate sidebars and tables.
Boldface references indicate photographs.

L

Labor, yoga helping with, 354
Lavender
   for calming effect before
      bedtime, 172
   for headache, 230
Leg Lowers, in mommy and me
   routine, **365**
Legs Sequences, 15-minute, 165,
   184, **185–93**
Legs Up the Wall
   for bloating, **337**
   how to do, 145, **145**
   for insomnia, **310**
   for jet lag, **237**
   in Legs Sequence, **193**
   for menstrual cramps, 18
   in P.M. Yoga Sequence, **175**
   for relaxation, 21
   in Relaxation Sequence 1, **319**
   variation, 145, **145**
Lemon
   Steamed Artichoke with Lemon
      Dip, 39
Light exposure, preventing sleep, 308
Liquids, avoiding, during yoga
   practice, 31
Little Tiny Package, in Core
   Sequence, **195**
Locally grown foods, 32–33
Locks, 14
Locust
   for better sex for men, **374**
   for hamstring strengthening,
      253–54

how to do, 131, **131**
   variation, 131, **131**
"Loka samasta sukhino bhavantu"
   mantra, 17
Lotus, for meditation, 329
Lotus Mudra, 296, **296**
Love, choosing fear vs., 9–10
Loving Embrace, for intimacy and
   sensuality, 381, **381**
Lower-back injuries
   causes of, 255
   relieving, 255–56
Lower-back pain
   from backbends, preventing, 128
   from core work, preventing, 138
   doing Sun Salutations with, 44
   from muscle tightness, 25
Lower-Belly Lifts, 151, **151**
   in Core Sequence, **195**
Low Lunge, for basketball players,
   275
Low Lunge Variation, for rock
   climbers, **285**
Lululemon, yoga clothing from, 19,
   390

M

Makarasana. See Dolphin
Malasana. See Garland
Manduka, yoga mats from, 391
Manifestation, 20
Manifestation journal, 20, 282
Mantras, 15, 17, 35
Maple Syrup Diet, 33

Mari, Giselle, 367, **367**
Marichyasana C. See Seated Twist
Marjaryasana. See Cow and Cat
Marrs, Leo, 245, **245**
Master Cleanse, 33
Mats, yoga, 19, 391
Meat
   choosing, 32–33
   eating, 16, 31
Meditation
   breathing during, 51
   calmness from, 9
   for focusing on crown chakra, 299
   for libido, 371
   preparing for, 6
   steps and tips for, 329
   for vertigo, 312
Meditation breath, 51
Melatonin
   for jet lag, 234
   for sleep, 308
Men, yoga for, 251, 286, **287–89**, 289
Menopausal symptoms, yoga for,
   333, 342, 342, **343–45**
Menstrual cramps, 18
Menstruation, yoga during, 17–18,
   341
Mental state of athletes, yoga
   improving, 252
Mentors, 9
Migraines, yoga relieving, 230,
   231–33
Miller, Jill, 253
Miller, Kia, 17, 242
Miller, MacKenzie, 223, **223**
Mind, yoga benefiting, 9–10